THE
PAINTED STREAM

THE
PAINTED STREAM

A RIVER WARDEN'S LIFE

ROBIN ARMSTRONG
with A.S.

J. M. Dent & Sons Ltd
London and Melbourne

To the memory of my father, Robert,
and to my children, Tamsin and Owen

Frontispiece: Wardbridge in May. The angler can only
dream about catching the sea-trout in the pool
below during the daylight hours. He will have to
wait until dark

Designed and produced by
BELLEW PUBLISHING COMPANY LIMITED
7 Southampton Place, London WC1A 2DR

First published 1985
© Bellew Publishing Company Limited 1985

This book is set in Baskerville
by Graphic Origination

J. M. Dent & Sons Ltd
Aldine House, 33 Welbeck Street, London W1M 8LX

British Library Cataloguing in Publication Data
Armstrong, Robin
 The painted stream: the life of a river warden.
 1. Estuarine biology—England—Plymouth (Devon)
 I. Title
 574.92'9'42358   QH138.P5/

ISBN 0 460 04702 7

CONTENTS

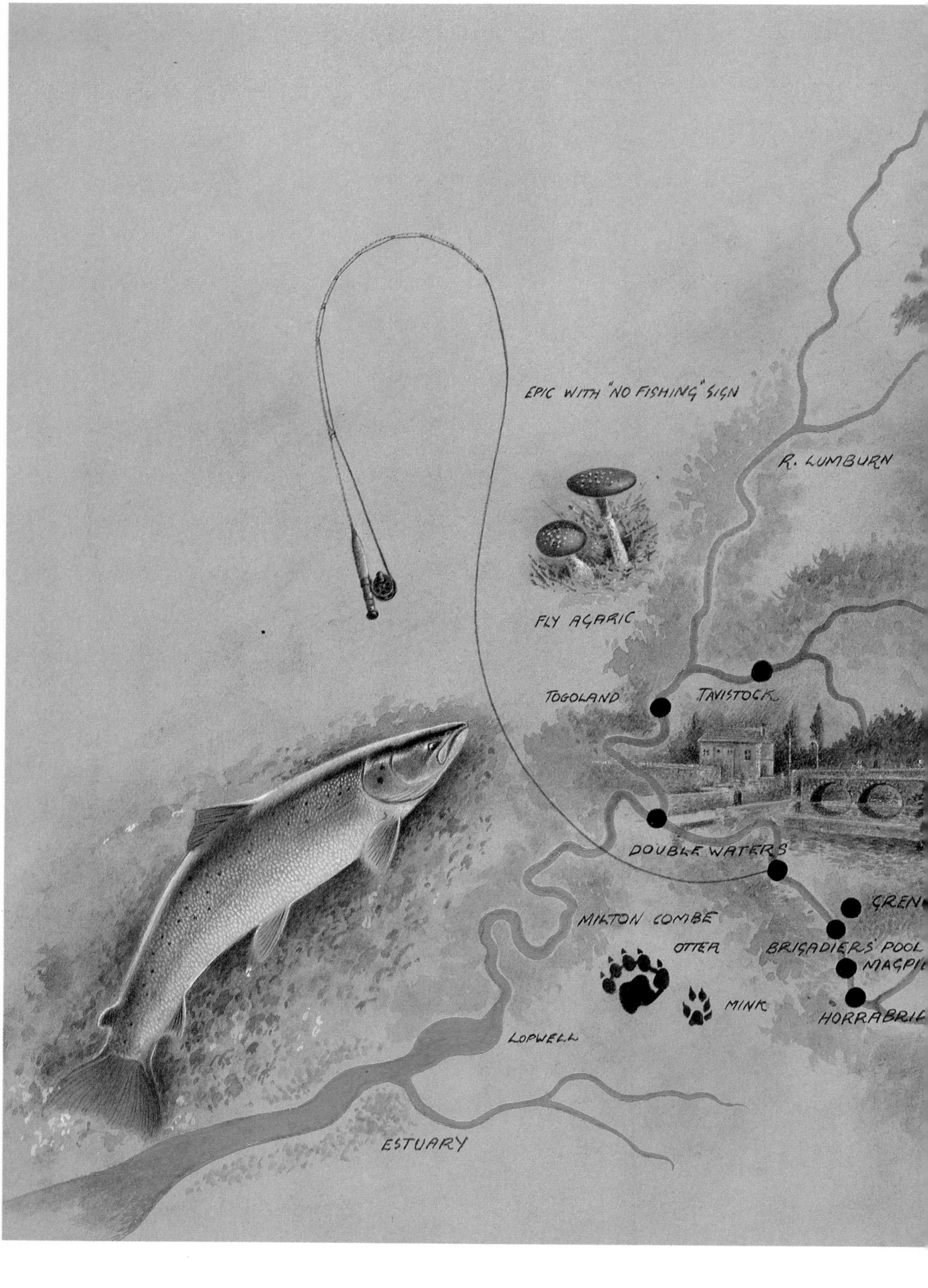

EPIC WITH "NO FISHING" SIGN

R. LUMBURN

FLY AGARIC

TOGOLAND   TAVISTOCK

DOUBLE WATERS

CREN

MILTON COMBE

OTTER   BRIGADIERS POOL

MAGPIE

MINK   HORRABRI

LOPWELL

ESTUARY

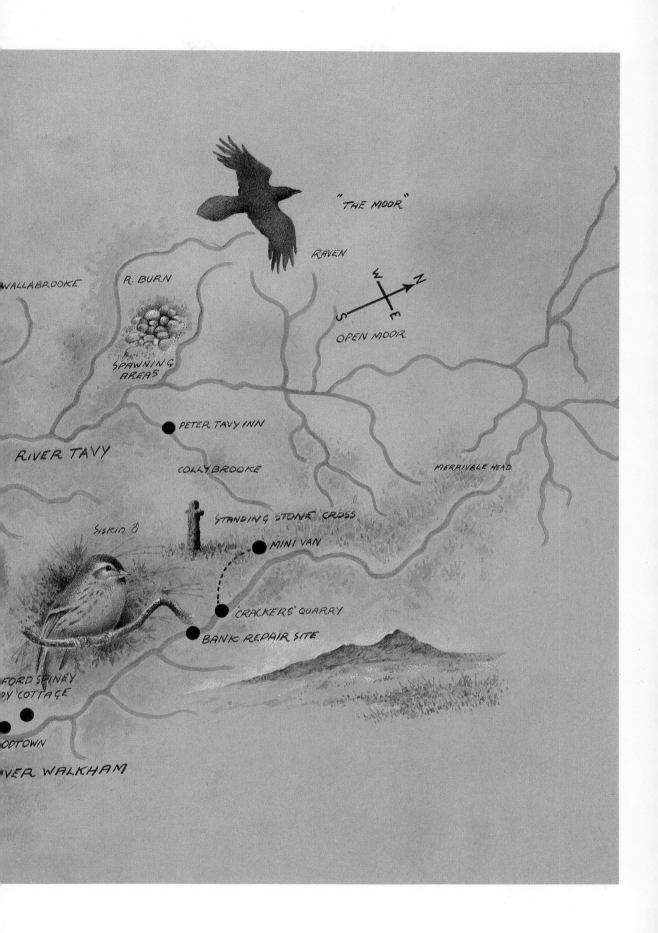

"THE MOOR"

RAVEN

WALLABROOKE

R. BURN

SPAWNING AREAS

OPEN MOOR

RIVER TAVY

PETER TAVY INN

COLLYBROOKE

MERRIVALE HEAD

STANDING STONE CROSS

SISKIN ♂

MINI VAN

'CRACKERS' QUARRY

BANK REPAIR SITE

FORD SPINEY
Y COTTAGE

ODTOWN

VER WALKHAM

AUTHOR'S NOTE

I should like to thank the following: for lending paintings for this book, Mr and Mrs C. Dare, Mr and Mrs J. Reynolds, Mr and Mrs B. Hulett; Mrs Rosalind Spedding for help in collecting the text; Devon Commercial Photos for permission to reproduce the photograph on the back flap of the jacket; my wife, Anne, for putting up with the almost constant use of the bath for soaking paper; the South West Water Authority for employing me in such a lovely area of England; and lastly, and above all, A.S.

FOREWORD

I am often asked what profession I would have liked to follow had I not become an actor and I always answer 'a river keeper'. Now I know what I have missed!

This is a book written and superbly illustrated by a river keeper, but it is about far more than keeping a river. Robin Armstrong is a fine naturalist, an acute observer of humanity, an artist of distinction and himself a fisherman. He writes of fish and fishing with style and delight, with sympathy and a happy sense of humour without sentimentality or anthropomorphism (though you are no fisherman if you can read the story of the two small boys and the salmon in Tavistock without a lump in the throat).

This is a REAL book and I cannot fault it for accuracy. Having lived on Dartmoor for years, I know the water of which he writes, and I have fished the upper Walkham for little moorland brownies and the Tavy on magic summer nights for peal. He gets it all RIGHT. (He even keeps his fly-tying material in that 'old black cash-box' – so do I!)

As for his illustrations, they are works of quite exceptional beauty, of nostalgia for any who know the West Country, and, again, of accuracy in observation.

This is a splendid, quite unputdownable book – one to place on the shelf with Arthur Ransome and Henry Williamson and Plunket-Greene. I am very honoured to have been asked to write this foreword.

MICHAEL HORDERN

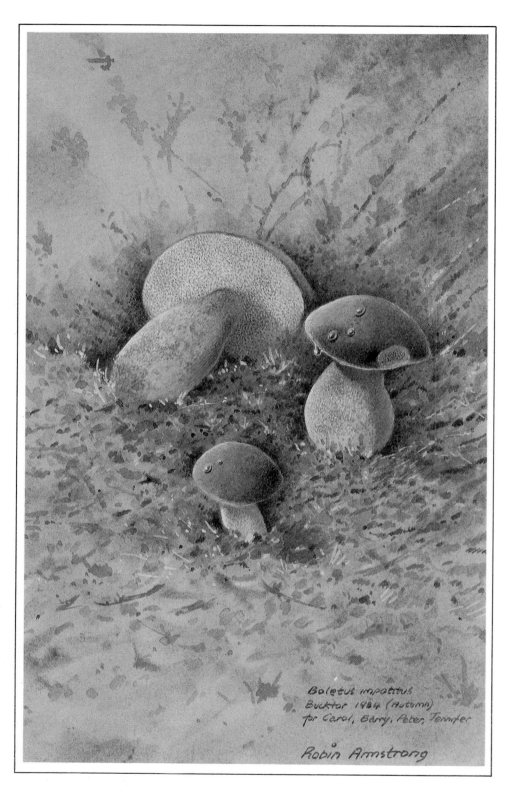

Boletus impotitus, Bucktor 1984 (autumn)

INTRODUCTION

'You'm a fair bit of a drawrer, Robbie . . .'

I suppose that's how it all started really. Sometimes it's a little difficult to understand the Devon accent at its ripest – rich, slow and thick like the local delicacy of clotted cream. Mind you, even those born and bred in the area could be forgiven for not fully understanding old Fred when he's supped more of his ration than usual. Fred is everyone's idea of the Local Character-cum-Oldest Inhabitant – a barrel-chested, furze-faced ancient in a faded smock and tattered sailor's cap whose mannerisms and speech are akin to that of a second-rate mimic impersonating Long John Silver. There's no parrot, though. Just Shandy, an arthritic old retriever with a fondness for the passing ankle and a bad-tempered bark, whose shambling gait matches that of his master on their perambulations through the little village of Peter Tavy.

It was a good night to be sitting round the fire at the pub. The Peter Tavy Inn, reputedly built in the fourteenth century, with yellowed ceilings and crudely sawn oak beams low enough to catch the unwary a sickening crack, is quaint enough and rustic enough to satisfy the most ardent of sightseers. But that particular evening was mid-week in winter and there was no sign of visitors in search of wholefood and real ale; instead there was a group of locals enjoying a drink and the pleasant and desultory conversation that goes with a warm fire and good company. I can't remember exactly who was there now, with the exception of Fred and the landlord, Paul, but whoever it was knew a thing or two about fish, for I had just completed a small watercolour of a brown trout and had brought it in to show Paul. No wild-life artist could wish for a better gallery than a popular country pub complete with knowledgeable locals who are experts on his subject-matter. At any rate, the picture met with some measure of approval for accurately portraying 'one o' they liddle tiddlers from up the Cleave' – a remark which pleased me greatly, for the painting was of a small brown trout (*Salmo trutta*) from the upper reaches of the river Tavy which runs off the high moor through Tavy Cleave. Gratified by this recognition, I put the picture to one side on a table and joined in the general conversation.

After a while, old Fred got up from his seat in the far corner and came over to the bar for a refill of mild and paused at the table on which the picture lay. He winked at me.

''Ad a few o' they in moi time,' he rumbled, looking at me slyly.

More than a few, I thought – and a salmon or two as well no doubt.

'Some big 'uns, too,' he said, reading my thoughts with a gap-toothed grin.

I shrugged. My vocation may be that of wild-life painter but it is a regrettably over-crowded profession with few possessed of sufficient talent and skill to evade the clutches of bank-managers and the like. A job is necessary to make ends meet.

''Course, it were all a long time ago.' A nudge in the ribs and another sideways look. Fred knew full well where my salary came from and who my employers were. 'Yer, a long time ago,' he sighed and reached for his new brimming tankard.

I kept my peace. It wouldn't be the first time a river warden of the South West Water Authority had held his tongue in a pub conversation. Poachers come in all shapes and sizes, and all ages – from sweet-sucking seven-year-olds to pension-drawing grandads.

Fred straightened up.

'You'm a fair bit of a drawrer, Robbie,' he said and took a long swig of mild. I moved forward and hastily moved the watercolour out of danger. I needn't have worried. Wiping his grizzled beard with the back of his hand, Fred said, 'Why don't 'ee write a book?'

I couldn't think of a snappy reply to the old man's question then, and I still can't now.

But this is the result.

Actually, I have to confess that this book was also written as a result of a professional misdemeanour. I was summoned to the presence of the head warden.

'It's about your notebooks,' he said, fixing me with a beady eye. 'They're a disgrace.'

I sat mute. The official pocketbooks that are issued to us are similar to those used by the police: small, lined notebooks containing some fifty pages with instructions for use and a copy of the Judge's Rules governing the procedure for arrest and the taking of statements printed neatly in the front.

'Have you read the instructions for use recently, and in particular para 8, section ii?'

'Er, is that the one about a pedlar's certificate not forming part of a pedlar's outfit or something?'

'No it is not. It happens to be the section that states that "no unnecessary, idle, or meaningless entries are made". Now look at your notebook–covered in sketches and drawings and whatever. These notebooks cost the Authority money, you know . . .'

My boss's bark is worse than his bite, but I began to see what he meant. The pages he was flourishing under my nose were covered with sketches of birds, animals, fishes, a twisted root exposed by the cutting action of water, a dragonfly, a section of stone bridge–anything, in fact, that had caught my fancy. My job as a river warden involves an awful lot of watching and waiting in the middle of some of the most beautiful countryside in England, teeming with all manner of flora and fauna, and not being able to record what I see is a kind of artistic cold turkey. However, since the Authority so conveniently issues me with notebook and pencil . . .

I apologized, promised to provide my own sketchbooks in future, and grovelled my way out.

When I got home that night I started to go through a pile of used notebooks. I had always used the sketches made on patrols or observation as a basis for most of my paintings. The delight of my job is that I am not only privileged to work at something I enjoy but it also keeps me constantly aware of the subjects that interest me as an artist. Later, in my potting-shed 'studio', I work those rough and ready sketches up into a completed study in pencil. Then, when I am satisfied, I transfer the work to a heavy water-colour paper for the completed painting.

It seemed to me that here was the basis for the book. Within the vandalized pages of the small pocketbooks were enough studies for a whole series of paintings, and, what was more, there was actually a substantial amount of written material–if I could decipher it from the scribbled sketches–that would form a foundation for the narrative.

This, then, is *The Painted Stream,* incidents in the life of one river warden working in one of the most beautiful parts of England–and I not only hope that my readers will like the book, I hope old Fred approves too.

Kingfisher

CHAPTER ONE

TWO CONSERVATIONISTS

I

ii.   In simple language inform the offender why he
is being arrested. This is essential, unless you are
prevented by the offender acting violently or running off

from 'ARREST PROCEDURE',
SWWA Notes to Water Bailiffs

'I'M a river warden and you are under . . . ' As I tried to get
the words out he twisted violently sideways, ducked, and
made for the hillside.

'Stop!' A waste of breath. Only one thing to do: go after him. Less
than fifty yards on, the pursuit began to seem a painful mistake.
The terrain was typical of most of the wooded valleys of Dartmoor:
very steep and rock-strewn with the ground under the oak, ash and
beech covered in scrub such as holly, hawthorn, blackthorn and
briar. To make matters worse, all this vegetation, combined with the
ever-present run-off water from the high ground, creates a soft
boggy mulch underfoot. If your upper body is not being held in
the thorn-studded embrace of a thicket, then for certain you are up
to your knees in black and treacly compost – and all this on a thirty-
degree slope.

He was about ten yards ahead and well above me. My wellington
boots and heavy waterproof jacket were not making things any
easier; every breath was a raw gasp, every step a muscle-wrenching
effort. It was soon obvious that my quarry was making better progress than I was. An exposed tree-root put an end to the chase; I
fell headlong, and could only watch, up to my wrists in soggy leaf-
mould, as he powered his way up the hillside. A blackbird, sentinel
of the woods, shrilled the alarm while a jay dipped through the
ancient trees screaming raucous abuse. Unheeding, the man continued his mad scramble upwards and was soon lost to my sight.

15

Loss of quarry, loss of dignity. I remained on hands and knees and listened to the sounds of flight dying away.

When the thumping in my chest had subsided to a manageable level, I cleaned myself up with a handful of fern and retraced my steps. Under the protective canopy of the bracken growing a few feet back from the river bank lay two salmon, silver elegance on the sparse grass. They were hen fish weighing around eight pounds apiece and the poacher had clearly only just claimed one, for it was still alive, gills and mouth gaping as it desperately struggled for breath in an alien environment. I removed the noose of soft brass picture-wire that had bitten cruelly into the salmon's body just behind the adipose fin and placed it in the stream, facing into the oxygen-rich water that tumbled between the great granite boulders. The fish twitched sluggishly between my hands as the process of revival began; indeed, it seemed that we regained our breath together, for, as the rapid beating of my heart slowed, the salmon gave a more positive twitch, flicking itself out of my hands and into the deeper waters of the pool. Back on the bank I kept an eye on the fish as I jotted down details of the abortive arrest in my notebook.

It was quiet under the trees, the only sound being the chuckle and splash of the river Walkham. I stared back up the hill and wondered where the poacher could possibly be heading; if he continued on his last-seen course, he would eventually come out on to open barren countryside, with nothing but the rocky tors and blanket bogs of Dartmoor stretching in front of him. Since he was a stranger to me in a sparsely populated area where public transport is virtually non-existent, it seemed reasonable to assume that somewhere in the vicinity there might be a car. I had seen no vehicle on my upstream journey except an aged tractor; if one existed, therefore, it could only be further upriver and on the opposite bank – for that was where the only track ran, built for access to a once busy quarry.

I picked up the remaining evidence and made my way across the shallows towards the track. The dead salmon, tucked inside the appropriately named poacher's pocket, swung weightily against my left hip and thigh, pulling uncomfortably across the shoulders of my jacket. As I walked, I examined the snare. It was unusual in that it was extremely well made, and the stick to which it was attached was a proper walking stick. The majority of poachers who use this method rarely take such care over their equipment: the noose is twisted out of any suitable flexible wire and the shaft is a sprit of hazel or similar, often cut on the spot so as not to attract attention.

This was an iron-shod hiker's stick, and the noose was attached to the bottom of it by means of a screw-on pipe-clip. Weals in the wood indicated that this was not the first time that the noose had been fastened on in this manner.

The derelict and grassed-over quarry revealed nothing more interesting than half-a-dozen Blackfaced sheep sharing their meagre diet with about the same number of rabbits. It was a peaceful scene in the mellow evening light and they seemed little disturbed by a human presence. I left them to their high tea and set off along the ancient rutted track which was covered with the green velvet nap of over-cropped grass. Where it slewed across the hillside to run parallel to the river, there jutted a boulder the height of a house. Set back from the track and embedded in the steep bracken-covered slope it is a prime vantage-point, the view from its top encompassing a stretch of nearly three miles of valley and hillside. I sat on the top and stared across, but the only movements I could detect were those of sheep and ponies grazing the lower slopes of a tor. The poacher must have stayed within the woods for there was no sign of unease among the animals, no herding together, no concerted flight from danger.

A thin and plaintive mewing came from above. High over my head a buzzard carved stately circles in the clear blue, searching for fading thermals and updraughts to lift him higher in his continual reconnaissance for prey. But now that the sun's rays no longer fingered the wooded valley floor, the invisible bubbles of heated air had dissipated, depriving the big bird of altitude. Perhaps it was

Soaring buzzard

warmth rising from the big rock that kept him wheeling overhead with outstretched wings, feathers at the tips opened like a splayed hand, searching for the minutest of rising air-currents. I envied him both his vantage-point and his powerful eyesight. From up there, I had little doubt, the buzzard's sharp eye would already have detected the escaping poacher moving among the stunted oaks of the tree-line opposite. Indeed, from up there the bird could see clear out of the county – not that the arbitrary boundaries of man would interest such a creature of the wild. To the east he could see across Lyme Bay where the red cliffs of Devon merge into the steep green combes of west Dorset backed by the Blackdown Hills. To the north, looking across the remote fastness of Dartmoor itself, his gaze would flick over the less bleak aspect of Exmoor to take in part of Somerset with the blue of the Bristol Channel pencilled thinly across the horizon; if it was exceptionally clear he might even discern a thin dusky line lying atop that water blue – the bulge of South Glamorgan. The natural border between Devon and Cornwall would show up clearly to the west – the River Tamar, from its estuary in the Plymouth Sound almost due south of us, north to its source less than five miles from the north coast. And south lay the deeply indented coastline stretching from Start Point to the east to the Lizard in the west, birthplace and graveyard of uncountable seafarers.

There is nothing fanciful about this panorama. A man I know, who regularly inspects the towering television mast at North Hessary Tor a couple of miles to the east of here, a thin pencil line etched vertically on the horizon, once described the 'champion view – five counties with the turn of your head'. I take his word for it; I feel distinctly queasy at the top of a household ladder. But the geographical sweep from aloft was of less interest to me (and indeed to the buzzard) than the view immediately below. I could follow the course of the Walkham through a patchwork of fields bounded by stone walls (monuments to numerous past generations who tried to eke a living from the thin and acid soil), and through an ancient woodland. Further downstream, rhododendrons grew in waxy-green profusion along the bank before the steep slopes opened out and scrub and wood gave way to less unkempt pasture. To be able to hang, apparently suspended in the air like the buzzard, and guard over the tumbling river and watch the desperate passage of the salmon and sea trout as they fought their way through riffle and rapid to gain the spawning grounds of the upper reaches seemed to me a highly desirable ability.

The predator above gave a mew of resignation and, failing to

Vixen Tor Quarry, one of the most striking tors I have seen

Scots pine

find further lift, sideslipped down the hillside towards the vantage-point of a tall Scots pine. With nothing to be seen on the opposing slope I followed his example and climbed down to the track.

I was annoyed with myself; an unknown poacher stealing fish worth over twenty pound 'under the counter' on my patch – and seeing me off into the bargain! Prime breeding stock, returning to the river of their birth for the first time in order to spawn. Since he was not one of my regular 'clients' I could hardly go and wait on his doorstep for his return. In irritation, I kicked at a granite chip on the path and sent it hurtling off into a shadowy patch of under-growth. There was a loud metallic clang. I stopped and looked closely; tucked in the bracken and sheltered by a large holly bush was a dark green mini-van. Bullseye! Not a local car, and in any case, why bother to conceal it so thoroughly?

I looked more closely. Under the dashboard was a 1:50,000 map of the area and beneath that was a snare, duplicate of the one already in my possession. The back of the van was cluttered with camping gear – rucksack, tent, sleeping-bag and stove – all of the highest quality: a salmon-subsidized holidaymaker no less. I had to admire his style, though; not only had he shown considerable speed and stamina in getting away, but he also displayed monumental cheek in disguising his activities, for the back windows of the van were almost obscured by conservationist stickers: 'World Wildlife Fund', 'Say No to Nuclear Power', Animal Rights', 'Royal Society for the Protection of Birds', plus the irrelevant and irreverent 'Wind-Surfers Do It Standing Up'.

Although I had found the transgressor's car, I was still not entirely sure what course of action to take. It seemed sensible to seek advice, perhaps even summon reinforcements – the stranger being bigger and undoubtedly more powerful than myself. My first attempt at arrest had been made in the heat of the moment – chance had led me to the spot where I had found him lying head down over the bank, seeking his prey among the water-washed and undercut roots of the Long Pool. I could wait by his car and try to arrest him again on his return, but in all honesty the plan didn't appeal to me. Dusk was approaching, and the long shadows cast in the valley were fingering their way to meet a chill mist spilling down from the high moor. He could easily escape again, quite pos-sibly giving me a good thumping into the bargain. Caution, if not downright cowardice, has always been my motto; reinforcements were definitely the order of the day. To shorten the odds still fur-ther in my favour, I now took a somewhat liberal interpretation of my powers of arrest and seizure. A water bailiff's authority in these matters is clearly defined by an Act of Parliament – the Salmon and Freshwater Fisheries Act 1975. Section 31, para (d) states that 'Any water bailiff appointed by a water authority and any person appointed by the Minister . . . may seize any fish and any instrument, vessel, vehicle or other thing liable to be forfeited in pursuance of this Act.' Well, I reasoned, if I could seize the whole vehicle, what possible objection could there be to me taking just a part of it?

Five minutes later, I was walking briskly along the grassy lane in the gathering darkness, the awkward bulk of the dead salmon counterbalanced in the other pocket by a far lighter, but infinitely more useful object, the rotor-arm.

II

The old granite quarry was last operating in the late 1950s, just one among the vast number that pockmark the moor. They now lie abandoned, visited only by the animals which crop the fast-encroaching grasses. Granite is the natural building material of the moor and the most common variety is blue-grey in colour, coarse in texture, hard and durable. Quarrying the stone is a fairly recent innovation, for local needs were generally satisfied by taking the surface granite in the form of boulders. The slopes of the tors (weathered granite outcrops) are strewn with such material in all shapes and sizes – a form of giant's pebble-dash known as clitter. Split with hammer and wedges and roughly dressed, the stone was carted away to build farmhouses, barns, and to clear and enclose fields. Quarrying was introduced as demand for granite grew, and the material was shipped far and wide – as the Breakwater in Plymouth Sound, Nelson's Column, and many other public works bear witness.

Jack 'Cracker' Smith, a nuggety little Yorkshireman, was once foreman of one of the largest of these now defunct works and, having married a local girl, took over a smallholding when the quarry closed. Weather-beaten but seemingly ageless, Meg and Cracker, now well into their seventies, still farmed on the bleak upper reaches of the valley, running a small flock of grey-faced, long-woolled Dartmoor sheep in company with a herd of equally shaggy Galloway cattle. Conveniently, their modest establishment lay beside the junction of the quarry track and one of the winding moorland roads.

Cracker was tinkering with the fuel pump of an ancient David

Fox studies from sightings during 1983

Brown tractor when I arrived in their yard. He straightened up and a spanner tinkled on to the rough concrete.

'Booger it. Yer just in time for tea, lad.'

I accepted gratefully, and asked permission to use the telephone. The old man cheerily waved his hand in the direction of the house and looked at me quizzically.

''Elp yersel', Robbie. Anyone we might know?' he added, with a conspiratorial wink. Little escaped his sharp eyes, so I told the story of the afternoon's events. He chuckled to begin with but was frowning when I told him of my accidental discovery of the mini-van.

''Oo'd believe it. Nice young lad he were, too. Talked proper and asked me if it were all right for him to have a scout around for a camp site, like. Not my land, but th'old Colonel don't mind, providin' I keep an eye out . . . '

Tut-tutting to himself about the iniquitous behaviour of the younger generation, he led me indoors. As I dialled the number of George, my boss, I reflected that there was no more righteous person than a convert – it was not so very long ago that my host had figured very highly on the bailiff's Most Wanted list.

Having been assured that support was on its way, I turned back into the cosy kitchen and the comforting warmth of the Aga. The old man handed me a steaming mug of tea, dark and strong like an ancient oak, and indicated a chair.

'Might as well wait for the booger 'ere. Meg's gone to Plymouth to visit 'er sister and won't be back 'till late. Booger 'as to coom through t'yard anyroad.'

Cracker's Yorkshire vowels were as strong as the day he had left to come south. He had once told me that the only difference between the small farmers of his own dales and those of the moor was to be found in their athletic ability.

'Both t'same. Hard as nails and can tell the weight of a beast to a pound and its worth to a penny – but down 'ere they can't play cricket.' As a Londoner and a Middlesex supporter I held my peace.

I sat in the chair and showed him my spoils. The snare he dismissed as being unnecessarily sophisticated, but the salmon came in for much admiration and he told me of the days when he first came to work on the moor, when fresh-run summer fish were commonplace in the upper reaches.

'From what I've been told, you had a fair few of those fish yourself. . . '

The lined face wrinkled into a grin of reminiscence.

'One or two, Robbie, one or two.' He reached over to the dresser for a blackened briar and tobacco pouch. 'Mind you, never got caught, but then things was different in those days, very different. No proper keepers like you Water Authority lads today, just a few private bailiffs, and all in all, a lot less fish. War was just over, y'see, and the rivers 'ad been poached silly by the squaddies an' the spivs. You could get big money for salmon in those days.'

'You still can,' I said, 'That's the problem.'

He waved at me impatiently from within his cloud of smoke.

'Ah mean proper money. People'd come from miles around to buy; not just restaurant-owners, but hotel-keepers, wide boys from London, even the bloody gentry. Why, Ah 'ad one magistrate's wife used to come to me regular–"Henny chance of a fish next Thursday, Mr Smith? Hai'm havin' a very himportant dinner party."'He chuckled and disappeared into another cloud of smoke. 'Mind you, Ah always reckoned the officer's messes were the best bet. Ah knew the ropes, y'see, since Ah were just demobbed; round the back, see the catering sergeant, and away yer went with a pocketful of brass. Grand days.'

He fell silent. I always enjoy old people's memories, in the same manner that I find the photograph albums of others fascinating; revelations of past times, only boring if forced upon one and in repetition. I prompted the old man by asking him whether he'd netted or snared the fish. He seemed mildly affronted.

'Ee, lad, don't yer know why Ah'm called Cracker?'

I shook my head.

'Well, Ah were in Sappers when Ah were in t'Army. Explosives, demolition an' all that. That were my trade, an' Ah were good, too, so that's why Ah went into quarryin' after demob.'

I stared at him in horror. 'You mean you blew the fish up?'

Seeing my expression, he leant forward and said, very seriously, 'Nay, lad, Ah didn't blow them up as yer put it, Ah just stunned them. The proper use of explosives is an art-form, see? If yer use the right amount of the right sort in the right place, yer could bring down Houses of Parliament with a teaspoonful. Anyroad, Ah were an expert, see, an' old Jim Trefusis, who were my first boss, said to me one day, "Smith, yer a cracker at blastin'. Why, Ah bet yer could blow open an oyster without givin' the booger an 'eadache." So after that Ah were always called Cracker.' He chuckled appreciatively.

Seeing that I was not entirely convinced of the ethics of exploding salmon, art-form or no art-form, he continued: 'Nowadays, not much dynamitin' goes on. Prevention of Terrorism Act sees to that. If they even catches you in possession without a licence, they chucks you in there an' throws away the key,' he said, with an emphatic nod in the general direction of Dartmoor Prison. 'No, days Ah'm talking about were just after the war, when it weer real cowboy country hereabouts. Nearly all the quarries had explosives magazines, an' most of them yer could open with yer Grannie's hat pin, not to mention what t'Army had left lyin' all over t'place. Yer couldn't move without summat goin' bang; hand-grenades flyin' around like cricket balls at Headingley, mortar shells and the like bein' used to blow tree-stumps an' crack boulders. Ah tell yer, it was bloody dangerous around here for a while.' He grimaced at the thought. 'Ah remember goin' to visit Meg's aunt when we was first courtin'. "'Ave a look at the clock, Cracker, it don't seem to be goin' so good," she says, so Ah opens the door of this old grandfather clock, an' Ah'm not surprised – one of the weights were missin' an' in its place were a rusty old Mills bomb hangin' by its pin! Must have been there since t'First World War.' Cracker shuddered at the memory. 'Still, yer were askin' about the fish. Like Ah said Ah were an artist. Ah used to study t'river real careful. Best places were deep little rocky pools – t'rock won't absorb blast like gravel, it's the concussion that does the trick, knocks 'em out, like. No bloody great bang like the other boogers, wi' fish-scales and guts endin' up draped in t'branches, just a gentle little thump and up they'd come, floatin' like great silvery feathers. Ah never did the same pool more'n once a run. Conservation, that's the trick – always leave some for next time,' he added with a wink. 'Now there's a car coming; likely be yer boss. Ah'll leave the kettle on t'stove, and if you want me, Ah'll be in end stable. Got a calf wi' squitters,' and he knocked out his pipe noisily against the coal hod and went outside.

III

George, my boss, and I leant against the gate leading to the track and waited. It was completely dark, and the claggy mist hung heavily in the still night air, showing itself in blurred haloes round the farmyard lights. I told George about Cracker's tales. He grunted in amusement.

'S'true, right enough. Old Sam, who used to be on this stretch of river years ago, told me that the sod blew a pool not ten minutes after Sam had passed. Didn't hear a thing – just felt a sort of bump underfoot; next thing he knew the water coming downstream was all muddy and discoloured with a few dead brownies floating in it. Three big fish there were in that pool, too. Cheeky devil!'

It occured to me that 'conservation' was a word of impressive

Tawney owlet. This one was brought in by some forestry workers, and I kept it and reared it until it was big enough to fly

flexibility if it could be used to describe my job and the past interests of old Cracker – not forgetting the activities of the owner of the sticker-bedaubed mini-van . . .

Long minutes passed in companionable silence – though even in the most remote sections of the moor at night, silence is a comparative term. Nearly always there is a background murmur from water trickling along a leat or welling up from an underground spring, or from the uneasy shuffle and low cough of hardy beast let out to graze the poor pasture, or the rustle in the bracken or heather as some small creature goes about its nocturnal business. Then there are the heart-stopping sounds, the shriek of an owl or the tortured scream of a vixen, for the high moorland is home to many predators, both feathered and furred. Surround the whole with impenetrable clinging mist and add a wind that whistles and reverberates round some of the strange misshapen rock formations and it is not difficult to understand why the ancient 'Land of Thunder' is home to so many legends and tales. Pixies, witches, ghostly hounds and the Devil himself are all part of moor mythology and, as such, familiar to the local children today. We supposedly live in pragmatic times but there is still a repository of belief among moor-folk – and not just among the young. Magic, as dispensed by 'white' or good witches, is not infrequently employed by some of the most hard-headed of the community, the upland farmers, to charm away warts or banish ring-worm in cattle.

Scoff if you like; ascribe such cures to chance, coincidence or psychosomatic causes and dismiss the myths and fables as the product of superstitious ignorance – but lie out on a bleak hillside on a pitch-black night and it is difficult not to let just the tiniest element of doubt enter the mind. Being an outsider, a 'furriner' or 'incomer' from London, I am something of a cynic, but there are one or two places along the sides of the upper river reaches where one senses a definite feeling of unease. Rings of standing stones, sites of ancient ritual and worship, are to be found in these sparse folds in the harsh ground. Who knows what rites took place within these granite-marked circles? Mind, the worst that has happened to me so far was when a badger stole my sandwiches!

Further flights of fancy were interrupted by a vigorous nudge in the ribs from George.

'Someone coming,' he muttered and pulled me back into the shadows. The roughly hewn stone of the ancient barn pressed uncomfortably into my back; inside, cattle lowed gently and shuffled their bedding uneasily. I strained to hear. There was a faint crunch of granite chippings as footsteps sounded on the track – not the brisk pace of the innocent or unwary, but the slow and cautious tread of one who suspects a trap.

Once again my imagination had led me astray in the darkness, for when my acquaintance of the afternoon emerged into the fogged light of the farmyard, it was apparent that his gait owed nothing to chariness but all to exhaustion. When I had first seen him he was dressed neatly in a green woollen checked shirt with rolled-up sleeves, lovat cords tucked into thick woollen socks, and a pair of walking boots. Three hours of being on the run had changed all that. His face and arms were covered with scratches, painful evidence of the dense thorn and bramble he had encountered. A crueller obstacle had evidently been barbed wire, for his left trouser leg had been ripped open across the thigh, and the weal of a deep abrasion showed redly against the skin. River and bog had obviously conspired to make his escape miserable for, from the waist down, his clothes clung wetly, showing dark streaks of peaty mud. I almost felt sorry for him.

I stepped away from the wall and out into the light. Taking him by the arm above the elbow, in the approved manner, I began again.

'I am a river warden and you are under arrest.' I was about to continue, when, for the second time that day, he interrupted me. Sweat streamed down his face from his matted hair and mingled with dirt and blood as he looked at me and said truculently: 'Why the **** didn't you say so in the first place?'

CHAPTER TWO

NOT ALL BIRDS AND BUTTERCUPS

I

'MORNING,' and with a slightly unsteady sloop-sloop of long thin skis, one of my more eccentric neighbours flailed past the back door to vanish down the steep snow-covered lane towards the river and its narrow stone bridge. I waited expectantly for the splintering crash, and was slightly disappointed to hear his voice cheerily greeting someone else on the other side of the valley a few moments later.

The snow lay around in wind-built hummocks, creating an alien panorama out of the once familiar landscape. Three days of gale-force winds had forced the white powder into drifts which blocked the narrow lanes and banked against the weather side of the walls and hedgerows so that it was difficult to tell where one field ended and another began.

Winter on Dartmoor is a bleak enough prospect without snow; with it, it becomes a time of starvation and death. A blizzard on the moor is not to be taken lightly; altitude lowers the temperature of the keen winds and the snow is driven on to the hard ground almost horizontally, the bare rocky slopes doing little to impede its progress. Animals huddle in the lee of stone walls or rocks, semi-comatose with cold and lack of food, only to find their shelter becoming a trap as the snow builds up and spills over to imprison and smother them. Birds, dashed about in the turbulent air, fall frozen to the ground, the remorseless white storm covering all trace of their short existence within seconds. Only in the thickest woods in the deepest valleys can sanctuary be found.

We humans huddle inside, bank up the fire, keep a wary eye on the flickering electric current, and congratulate ourselves on our foresight in taking advantage of that special offer on baked beans

29

in the supermarket last week; or at least some of us do. Those who farm, and have managed to bring in the stock before the storm, begin the almost continuous routine of feeding and mucking-out, anxiously watching food stocks dwindle. Emergency deliveries of animal feed by helicopter are not unknown around here.

The blanket of white is not, however, comprehensive. Gaze up at the tors and an almost lunar landscape is revealed. The wind scours the massive rocks and boulders, leaving a thin dusting of snow to clog the meagre vegetation while exposing the stone. Chiaroscuro, a vista of black and white.

With the easing of the wind the picture changes dramatically– for the humans. Children, secure in the knowledge that there will be no school for days, perhaps even weeks, tumble down the slopes, shrieking at top voice, and even the adults deign to unbend; my neighbour of the morning was not the only one to rush around in the belief that he is Captain Scott reincarnated.

A watery light filtering through the pale overcast encourages the birds harbouring in the surrounding woodland to venture out in search of food. The dazzling new face of the land has little to offer them. Some, however, are more adaptable than others; pied wag-tails and robins, imbued with a deep knowledge of human beings and their ways, gather round the farmyards and pens watching the milling herds churn the pristine whiteness into a steaming muddy sludge and exposing all sorts of grubs and insects. Other birds sur-vive through their knowledge of even colder regions; the migratory woodcock, for instance, which ranges from the Arctic wastes of Rus-sia and Scandinavia, seeks sustenance in the valley bottoms where springs show darkly as a stain amid the snow, and moisture softens the hard soil for a probing beak. The woodcock is a regular visitor of almost impeccable punctuality to the valley, arriving with the first full moon in November and departing the first week of March. Even for these experienced birds, conditions are hard and their departure date may have to be put forward. But for most of the smaller birds the desperate business of living in a world that has literally changed overnight may prove too much; in these times the only beneficiaries are often the carrion-eaters.

I had duly fed bird-tables and baskets over the last few days and was naturally delighted by the grateful display put on by the diners –although their table-manners left something to be desired. In the fir copse running beside the lane that leads to the river there was something of a rarity–a family of siskins that had stayed to breed, and I was relieved to see the cock and hen feeding, along with a

The church at Sampford Spiney

Nuthatch

nuthatch who undoubtedly had a severe headache from trying to hammer at bark that was the consistency of tempered steel.

We were fortunate; our home is by the hamlet of Sampford Spiney on the western side of the moor, an area of ancient woodland that offers a modicum of shelter from the worst of the weather. Nevertheless, the lanes and tracks were choked with snow and it would be some time before even a tractor could get through.

Sheltered we might be, but it was still bitterly cold, and frozen particles of snow swirled in the air like diamond dust. Down by the river icicles hung over the dark fast-moving water. With no chance of leaving the immediate confines of home for a day or so, it seemed like a good chance to catch up on correspondence.

II

I collect fishing tackle – or, rather, I used to, for as an estate tenant I was recently offered the opportunity to buy my cottage outright, an opportunity too good to miss and so the collection was sold in the effort to raise money. Nevertheless, I have hopes of starting again, and, like all avid collectors, I pore over the saleroom catalogues and the classified section of the angling press. My speciality was fishing reels: those made by the famous firm of Hardy Brothers of Alnwick in Northumberland and, in particular, fly-reels made around the beginning of this century – simple mechanisms, but made with all the precision and care of a Swiss watch.

Before I sold the collection I had made the acquaintance of a fellow enthusiast from Herefordshire, had swapped various items and had kept up an occasional correspondence ever since. Recently he had written to me about his son and, flatteringly, asked my advice – I was flattered since my own son is hardly two yet, and the little I know about children is confined to the messier and noisier aspects of their behaviour.

'As you know, James is now fifteen and shows little interest in academic subjects [that sounded familiar] yet displays a considerable talent for drawing and is fascinated by anything to do with natural history [even more familiar!]. His only other interest seems to be fishing. We were wondering if you could help us, since your way of life would seem close to James's ideal. Just how do you become a water bailiff, and what qualifications are necessary?'

I got out pen and paper. My way of life was certainly my ideal, but whether it was James's or not remained to be seen. The biggest difference between the two of us was geographical; as a lad I had been brought up in and around the sprawling council estates of south London – a far cry from my friend's son who lived beside the lush banks of the river Wye and at a considerable distance from any sizeable town. None the less, the other details matched in every respect . . .

The only two subjects for which I had shown the slightest ability at school had been art and natural history; my exercise-books were always recognizably mine, since every cover and every margin was festooned with amateurish yet finely detailed sketches of British flora and fauna – mostly gathered from the pages of that excellent series of field-guides so dear to every schoolboy's heart – the Obser-

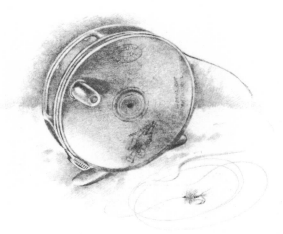

ver books. I read and re-read those little books from cover to cover, swapping those that I did not want, such as *Aircraft* and *Ships*, for the likes of *Grasses, Sedges and Rushes* and *Freshwater Fishes of the British Isles*. I suppose my schoolmates must have thought me more than a little barmy to be more interested in the feeding habits of the willow warbler than in the number of engines carried by a Vickers Viscount. My head was stuffed full of facts that no one else could give a row of beans about.

At the age of fifteen I left school and got a job as office boy in the art department of an advertising agency. As I changed the illustrators' water-pots, ran various errands for them ('Five bob each way on Lucky Lad in the 2.30 at Lingfield – oh, and get us a packet of fags while you're about it') and sharpened the pencils, it hardly seemed as if my artistic talents were being appreciated, and, what was worse, the environs of central London were as nothing compared to the magical delights of the countryside. I used to read many of the glossy magazines that came through the agency, particularly those that dealt with rural life, and it was one of these that gave me the idea of becoming a gamekeeper. This was not something that I had previously considered, but the more I thought about it, the more it made sense: healthy outdoor life, an unparalleled knowledge of country lore, a deep and abiding respect for the ways of nature, and a position of repute among one's fellows – or so the article led me to believe. I could picture myself, tweed-suited, gun over arm and dog at heels, striding along the rides (although I was none too sure what a ride was). I began to answer advertisements in the classified sections of the country magazines while the office looked on at my efforts with uncomprehending amusement.

Willow warbler

Initially, my efforts met with little success; hardly surprising since my only acquaintance with country pursuits was a passion for coarse fishing. Then one day I wrote to the Game Conservancy Board which informed me, almost by return of post, about a vacancy for an under-keeper on the Cowdray Estate at Midhurst in Sussex. An exchange of letters led to an appointment to meet the Head Keeper, Mr Holman, at Cruft's Dog Show the following week.

Suit pressed, shoes cleaned and hair well slicked down, I sallied forth to Olympia desperate to impress. If the interview was something of an anti-climax, Sid Holman was not. Big, beefy and red of face, he looked every inch a head keeper in a three-piece brown tweed Norfolk suit complete with matching deerstalker. Thick brown woollen socks with red tabs ended in a pair of old-fashioned brown ankle boots. Stammering, I introduced myself to him. He said nothing in reply, but merely leant on his thumb-stick and regarded me unblinkingly. I began to panic. What was wrong? Wasn't he going to ask me any questions? Had all my foraging in Bromley Public Library been wasted? He stared down at me, seemingly oblivious to the continuous din of yapping, barking, whining and growling interspersed with garbled echoing announcements over the public address system. Eventually he grunted.

'You'll do,' he said, and from one of his capacious pockets took out a battered notebook and a stub of a pencil, and carefully began to write. 'I'll pick you up at Pulborough station in a fortnight's time at ten o'clock. Here's the telephone number of the Estate Office. They'll tell you what you'll need and send a ticket. Afternoon.'

He turned on his heel and walked towards the area assigned to working dogs, leaving me in a complete daze. I couldn't believe it. I was going to be a gamekeeper. I was going to live in the country. All my dreams seemed to be coming true . . . In a joyous daze I turned on my heel and immediately trod on one of the less appealing aspects of canine life.

As a result of what must be one of the shortest job interviews on record, I was standing two weeks later on the platform at Pulborough in a state of nervous anticipation. Imagine a lanky sixteen-year-old, dressed in a loud and obviously second-hand sports jacket, ill-fitting corduroy trousers, and enormous black boots – the object of some contention between my father and me. Whereas I 'knew' that all gamekeepers wore brown boots, Dad had merely pointed out that the local branch of Millets stocked only the black variety and that the clothes list from the Estate Office said nothing as regards to colour. I had sulkily given in. Mind you, I felt there was a certain degree of compensation in the matter of my hat. Pur-chased with some of my hard-earned savings, it was the nearest thing that Bromley could offer in terms of a genuine deerstalker. A checked tweedy contrivance, somewhat overlarge, it rested on my ears like a large and hairy pudding-basin. I was inordinately proud of it.

Sid Holman appeared through the ticket barrier. Monosyllabic as before, he greeted me with a brief 'Mornin' and wheeled my bicycle, brought down in the guard's van, towards the carpark, leaving me to stagger behind clutching Dad's old kit-bag, into which had been crammed all my worldly possessions. In the carpark there stood – wonder of wonders! – a land-rover. I shall never forget those few miles that we drove between Pulborough and Midhurst. It was February, and the brown swollen river Arun had overflowed its banks and flooded the neighbouring water-meadows. A weak sun reflected off the sheets of water and lit the bare trees from beneath with a mellow light, and as we drove along the narrow Sussex lanes it seemed that wildlife was everywhere. Mallard and teal dabbled busily in the grassy shallows, while rooks chattered and squabbled in the tall elms (Dutch Elm disease had yet to make its dreaded presence felt). Pheasants scratched among the winter wheat. The biggest thrill of all came when we passed beside the walled deer-park that encloses Petworth House and I caught a glimpse of the herd within.

Sid spoke little on the journey, other than to tell me the names of various villages and landmarks (Fittleworth, Byworth, Petworth, Tillington, Little Common, Long Wood, Benbow Pond . . .). I paid little attention and shivered with excitement like a spaniel in antici-pation of sport. On arrival at his cottage I was greeted kindly by his wife and shown my room. I unpacked – yet another novel experi-ence – and before long was standing downstairs in working rig of overalls and gumboots, a very model of a keen and enthusiastic apprentice gamekeeper. It was something of a let-down, therefore, to be handed an axe and told to go outside and split logs.

It was a daunting task made worse by ignorance – something to which I could not possibly admit. Within half an hour I had blunted and chipped the blade on the concrete, pulled all the muscles in my shoulders, blistered the palms of my hands and irre-trievably stuck the axe-head in a particularly knotty piece of wood. The few split pieces made a pathetic pile alongside their untouched brethren. Frustration and despair brought me close to tears; if I could not manage the simplest of rural chores, how on earth was I going to cope? Eventually, Sid came to my aid and

Pheasant, partridge and teal – memories of Petworth

showed me the use of wedges and sledge, and how to swing the axe so as to make the very weight of the tool work in one's favour; if he found anything odd in the fact that I seemed so hopeless, he did not say so.

That afternoon, Mr Holman – as I was told to call him – took me round that area of the estate that I was to work in. We visited the breeding and rearing pens, walked the hedgerows and copses, and called on neighbouring tenant farms. It was dark by the time we returned home. Exhausted and bewildered, I ate little and staggered off to bed. But worse was to come. It seemed that my aching body had not been huddled under the blankets for more than half an hour, when I was shaken awake.

'Kettle's on the boil' said my new boss, and clumped out of the room. Blearily, I looked at my shiny new Timex (a going-away present from my parents) and could hardly believe what I saw. Five o'clock in the morning – it was still pitch black outside! Before long I was struggling in the darkness, bowed under the weight of two large buckets filled to the brim with corn, stumbling across the unfamiliar terrain of a ploughed field in the direction of an unknown hedgerow. I remember it being bitterly cold, and the wet, newly-turned soil seemed to clutch at my every step. After a few

Barn owl

yards the hedgerow marked the boundary of a small wood, and I had been instructed to feed into a small ride which led to a trapping pen – instructions which I only barely understood. Under the dark loom of the trees, my surroundings were both unfamiliar and menacing. The natural historian in me told me that the scratchings and rustlings which seemed to surround me in the darkness were no more than the sound of the pheasants emerging from the undergrowth in search of the corn, and that the occasional loud, flapping, crashing sounds were merely other pheasants coming down from their roosts; but the townsman was not so convinced, and when a barn owl let out a piercing screech, seemingly inches from my left ear, all my urban instincts asserted themselves. In a panic, I blundered out of the wood, scratched and whipped by briar and twig, and lurched into the field – only to trip over a furrow and fall full-stretch in the claggy mud.

III

Of course, young James wouldn't have any problem with the simplest tasks that had reduced me to a quivering jelly, and anyway, he wanted to become a water bailiff, not a gamekeeper. The only lesson to be learned from my initial experience was: beware the dangers of romanticizing. Although I saw myself as a gamekeeper striding down a ride, clad in tweeds, gun under arm and dog at side, that was not really *my* image – it was a composite, taken from

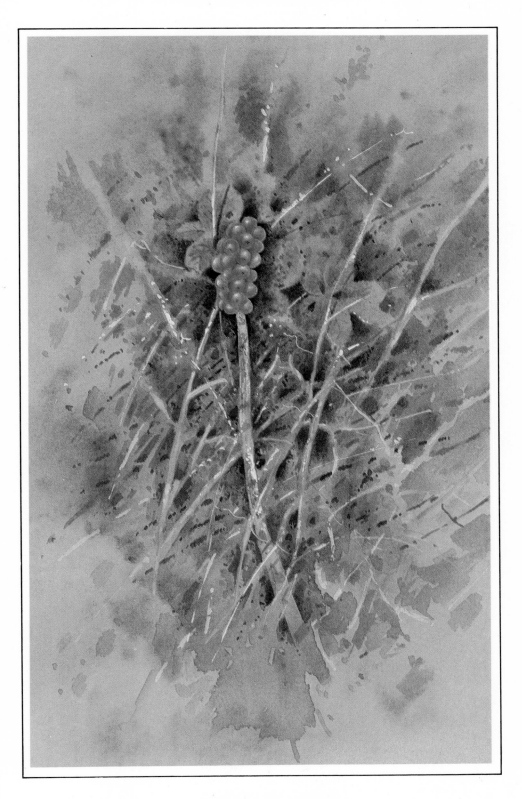

Lords and ladies (August)

the descriptions of others. There was nothing in the picture to suggest hard manual labour or weather that was anything other than the finest of spring days. Since there was no reality or substance to my illusion, it was easily shattered. If I could not accomplish the most basic task without help or instruction, how could I possibly succeed? I had decided to become a gamekeeper on a whim; merely as a means of getting myself out into the countryside. I had also mistaken a vocation for a job.

Those first twenty-four hours remain very clear in my memory, etched there by the diamond tip of uncomprehending despair. It seemed that every simple task that I put my hand to was doomed to failure; it was not merely knowledge that I had to acquire, but also the basic skills to go with it. Perhaps most important, though, was the realization that it was not just a new job that I had embarked upon, but an entirely new way of life – something that was very difficult to understand as a teenager. Probably the hardest thing to assimilate was the idea that the job was never over, that, unlike the routine found within a city, there was no clocking-on and no clocking-off. Of course, I knew that not everybody had a nine-to-five job – my dad, for instance, worked all sorts of odd hours, but that was ascribed to 'shift-work' or 'overtime'. What I found so difficult was the notion of living over the shop, that at any hour of day or night, regardless of the hours that I had already put in, I would be expected to turn out if things weren't quite right.

Life on a large estate appeared rigid and formal, almost feudal in its outlook, and the pace slow but never-ending. It was a hierarchy with his lordship at the top, and, it seemed to me, Armstrong at the bottom. I was taught to raise my cap and call people 'sir' or 'madam'; I couldn't understand it – I thought I had left all that sort of nonsense behind when I had left school. I would become sulky and mulish at the slightest reprimand, and, with all the originality of a teenager in the sixties, I began to rebel. My cockney accent became broader and I began to call those around me 'mate' or 'moosh' (though not, I hasten to add, Mr Holman – my rebellion was not of a courageous nature). As the daylight hours lengthened I began to stay out later, finding companionship with other dispossessed city-lads from neighbouring towns and villages, and, in consequence, found the early-rising routine more and more of a struggle. Naturally, my work suffered. In order to catch up, I skimped on feeding and maintenance and became slapdash. The afternoons when I was supposed to check snares and traps and deal with vermin such as magpies, jays, stoats, weasels and foxes became something of a farce. The fact that I had realized an ambition and was free to wander with a gun and dog over thousands of the most beautiful acres in the south of England meant nothing any longer. The initial thrill of being allowed to handle a real shotgun quickly wore off, and I found the lectures on safety and maintenance tedious and interminable. With the self-opinionated arrogance of youth I decided the whole thing was pointless – killing was wrong so why should I carry a gun anyway? The vermin began to increase on my patch while I used the afternoons to catch up on my sleep or to sketch in the hedgerows.

The end was not long in coming, and, like the misery of the first day, it is sharply imprinted in my memory. Late down, as usual, I was lacing my boots when Sid said, 'When you fed the pens, get your best clothes on.'

I mumbled a reply and went out into the chill morning dawn to feed the pheasant poults (young). There was nothing unusual about Sid's instructions, for he often took me with him to visit neighbouring keepers, farmers and suppliers. I always enjoyed these visits, rattling around in the old land-rover, being introduced as the new 'lad' and meeting people and seeing places that I had never suspected existed. Lately, these trips had become something of a rarity, so it was with considerably more enthusiasm than usual that I collected the feed, kept in huge galvanized bins to discourage rats, and went out to give the peeping hordes their breakfast.

Back at the house, I paused on my way upstairs. 'Where're we going, Mr Holman?' I asked.

There was an awkward pause. Mrs Holman busied herself with frying slices of bread on the Aga, while her husband concentrated on the laborious job of shaving himself using an old-fashioned cut-throat razor and a broken mirror propped up on the mantelpiece. After a couple of slow and deliberate scrapes, he flicked the suds off the razor and said, 'Not we, young Robin, just you. You're going home, back to London.'

The feeling of rejection was like a physical blow; the room darkened and I literally could not breathe for a moment or two.

'Wh-why?'

He sighed and put down his shaving implements.

''Cos you're doing us no good, and yourself no good. Now go along and pack and I'll take you to the station.'

Every step I took from then on was like wading through treacle, though the feeling was far from sweet. The journey to the station was a complete antithesis to my arrival six months previously. The countryside passed by in a dull blur as I sat staring blindly through the insect-spattered windscreen. At the station my ticket was

bought for me and I was led on to the platform with my bike and
kit-bag.

Once on the train, the wretched feeling of rejection began to
turn to self-pity and tears. It was the first time in my life that I had
been told that I wasn't wanted – and it hurt, God! how it hurt. The
only consolation came from Sid's parting words.

"Tisn't for ever, son,' he'd said gently. 'You've just got to go away
and grow up a bit. Life in the country isn't all liddle birds and buttercups y'know; it's hard graft and you just ain't cut out for it. We've
both made a mistake,' he continued kindly. 'Now off you go, but
come back one of these days and show me that I'm wrong.'

That was over twenty years ago. The years passed and eventually
I did go back to prove him wrong, to show him that I was still a
keeper, though of fish, not fowl – but it was too late, for the old man
had long gone. The cottage in the woods, with the window frames
and doors painted in the estate colour of dark yellow had been
converted and enlarged and was now a smart farmhouse standing a
little way back from a new dual carriageway running between
Petworth and Midhurst.

I had lasted only six months – but it had been a salutary shock to
the system. At first I was bitter and resented the fact that I had been
given very little warning of dismissal, but on reflection I think Sid
was right. It might have been different if I had been brought up the
son of a keeper – but I doubt it. I gave up the moment my romantic
image shattered, the moment I was shown a pile of logs and an axe.
If I was to have a vocation I had to show aptitude – the opportunities were there but I ignored them; Sid probably had his doubts
about me from the first day and he gave me every chance, but I let
him down.

I went back to emptying water-pots and sharpening pencils – but
at a different agency.

IV

I couldn't see how any of this was going to be of any use to my
friend's son. At fifteen, the virtues of hard work and taking everything one step at a time are dinned into you morning, noon and

Common sandpiper. This bird used to breed here but now appears mostly as a
passage bird

night. The problem, I realized, was that I was none too sure how to become a water bailiff myself; unlike the gamekeeping episode it was something I had eventually just drifted into.

Two years in London, followed by a brief round-the-world excursion courtesy of the Merchant Navy had done nothing to change my ambition to live and work in the country; but I was reluctant to make the move – a case of once bitten, twice shy. I sublimated the ambition by spending nearly every weekend bird-watching, fishing, sketching or just generally tramping round rural areas within an easy train-ride from London.

The expression 'twitcher' had not been invented in those days – enthusiastic bird-watchers were just classed with other amiable loonies obsessed with harmless pastimes – but if you take into account the lack of equipment (no telephoto lens or motor-drives, no high-powered binoculars or telescopes, no vehicles with CB radio) our behaviour was little different from the modern, mechanized ornithological zealot. It was little more than a grown-up game of I-spy; the competitive element entering strongly into proceedings – one particular craze was trying to do the 'ton'; an expression borrowed from motorcycling contemporaries and implying that one had seen a hundred different species in a day. I never managed it myself, but I knew several fellow-watchers who had – or who said they had.

Since my other hobby was fishing, I nearly always set off on these expeditions armed with a comprehensive assortment of tackle, on the grounds that if the birds weren't showing, then the fish might be biting. It was on such a weekend in early May that I finally saw the light. With some companions, I was roaming the tidal mud-flats and shingle beaches of Pagham Harbour in West Sussex. It was a clear, if chill, evening and my three interests were being more than adequately catered for: on the seaward side of the spit that protects the entrance to the silted harbour I had set up a rod and rest in the hope of catching supper – we had camped in a field near Selsey a mile or so away – and was spending my time attending to the tackle and climbing back over the dunes to watch and sketch the birds dabbling and flying over the flats. Looking west across the harbour from the spit, I saw, reaching across from the horizon, the beginnings of a gentle and exquisite sunset; no Wagnerian canvas of rolling oranges and flaming reds, but a wash of pinks and blues with a hint of palest apple-green. The breeze had stilled for the evening and against this pastel backcloth wheeled the guardians of the marshes, the redshank, their bell-like piping ringing through the cool moist air. Restless birds, they swung ceaselessly overhead,

Redshanks at Lopwell

Redshank

hovered and fluttered over the saltings, and settled – only to take off and repeat the process all over again moments later.

My companions were equally restless; replete after a long day of ornithological activity, their interest was being diverted by thoughts of birds of a different kind – and the fact that it was a good hour past opening time.

I was looking at my sketch of the redshank silhouetted against the sunset and wondering if perhaps some blades of marsh grasses in the foreground would improve the composition when one of them said, 'Tell you what, Rob, if you let me have that picture, I'll pay for your pints this weekend. Now come on, we're wasting valuable drinking time.'

Definitely an offer not to be refused. I tore the page off the cartridge pad, handed it over, and set off through the marram and across the shingle to collect my tackle and our supper – dabs, if I remember rightly.

Wandering along in the wake of the others, I suddenly realized what had happened – I had sold a picture! Oddly, for one who worked in a commercial studio – albeit as glorified messenger boy – the thought of selling my work had never consciously occurred to me. I wondered if I could do it again; I decided to sound out the others.

Over the second round I broached the subject. Their reaction was enthusiastic, if somewhat surprising.

'We always thought you did sell 'em. Daft as a brush not to. Here, give us the pad an' we'll see what the punters in the saloon bar think.' Before I could protest, my sketchbook was whisked away and

46

Male dragonfly. I see clouds of these lovely insects on the river in summertime

four sharp-witted young Londoners, commercial instincts alerted, vanished into the crowd.

The little dabs lay uneaten that night. It was a fry-up in a local café courtesy of R. Armstrong, wild-life artist, and the punters in the saloon bar. The staggering sum of £14 12s 6d signified the start of my new career.

Not that life was all fry-ups and free pints after that. I took the advice of the artists in the advertising agency and began to submit my work to magazines, and over the first year collected enough rejection slips to fill a scrapbook. Still, my pictures sold in pubs and local galleries on our weekend trips and I slowly began to build up a profitable sideline. The studio advice was good and practical: 'Go to art school for a year or so and learn technique, then become a commercial artist like us and continue wild-life painting as a side-line – that way you won't starve.' Sound advice, but not quite in accordance with the dream which had substituted the tweeds and gun for paint-stained smock and palette; at least this time I had some idea of the practicalities involved – even, I thought, the hardships; after all, didn't I have the rejection slips to prove it?

Uncertain and unsure, my mind was made up one bank holiday weekend, on our furthest expedition yet – all the way from London to sunny Torquay. Fishing from the harbour wall on the second day, I fell into conversation with a fellow-angler, a tall, cadaverous man who told me that he was after conger. With all the assurance and experience of my nineteen years I told him exactly what he was doing wrong and how inadequate his equipment was. He patiently heard me out then introduced himself; to my horror, I discovered that I had been lecturing one of the best-known fishing writers of the day. Mind you, I was so cocky in those days that my embarrassment lasted only moments . . .

We leant against the railings and talked, oblivious of the milling crowds of holidaymakers and ever-hopeful gulls. To be honest, I was the one doing the talking while Ewan Clarkson patiently listened. I think no matter how close one is to one's parents there comes a point in most adolescent lives where the understanding and sympathy of another adult can be of enormous benefit. Ewan provided that sympathy and understanding in my case; he also provided sound practical advice and help as well. He was the first person I had met who fully understood and encouraged my passion for the countryside. Within days, I had left my job in London and had moved down to Devon. I shall always be eternally grateful to Ewan and his wife Jenny for their kindness and hospitality – for I stayed with them and their family for over a year.

It was Ewan who introduced me to Dartmoor, and from the moment I first set eyes on that bleak and seemingly inhospitable tract of land I was hooked. Twenty years later, the lure is just as difficult to explain. I was then an 'incomer', an outsider, a Londoner, with no previous connection with either Devon or the moor. At the time I dismissed the feeling as being a reaction to the wildness and freedom of the place; being more used to the restrictions of the Home Counties where the pressures of agriculture and population have led to a more formal landscape. Later I realized that this was nonsense – I had never really felt restricted in the countryside close to London, despite the more intensive farming and the greater numbers of people, and I remain just as fond of the woodlands, downs and sandy heaths as I ever was; the attraction of the moor was something far deeper. My father was a Border man – an Armstrong among many – and perhaps there is an echo of the fells among the high tors and fast-flowing streams. Whatever the reason, I am not the first, nor shall I be the last, to fall for the moor's rugged charms.

V

None of this introspection was helping young James to become a water bailiff. I gazed out of the window: no inspiration there. The watery sun had long receded into the ominously dark sky and a probing breeze was just beginning to stir the tree-tops showing darkly against the backcloth of white. It looked as though we were in for another heavy fall within the hour.

I recalled another winter spent in chilling numbness in a more remote part of the moor. For students of industrial archaeology, Powder Mills is a fascinating site; lying in a bleak and windswept landscape some two miles to the north-east of Princetown, close to the Cherry Brook, it was once a thriving settlement employing over a hundred souls. By the time I arrived there, there was little sign of such a community; there remained but four cottages, a farm, and the ruins of the factory. There is sound reason for the isolation – the powder ground between granite mill-stones rotated by water-power was gunpowder, and accidents were not infrequent. The sole visible legacy of this dramatic past is an old mortar that was used for proofing the powder: the strength of the powder being determined by the distance a given amount would propel an iron or granite ball.

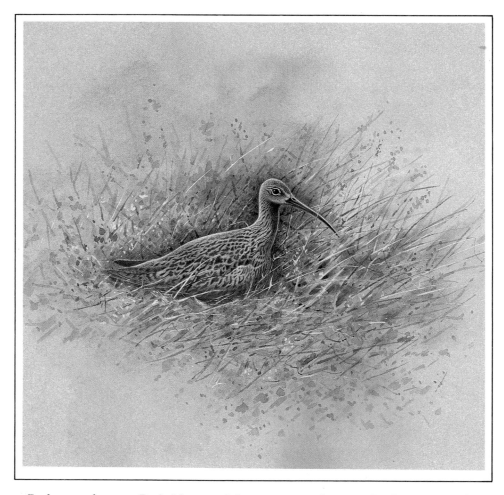

Curlew on the nest. Probably one of the most evocative sounds of summer is that of male curlews on the nesting grounds

To this now peaceful spot I moved. For two years I survived on the proceeds of painting and illustration – but only just. The rejection slips no longer came through the post with monotonous regularity – there was even a commission or two – but the world of the wild-life art *aficionado* had yet to beat a path to my door. By tucking myself away in the isolation of Powder Mills it was hardly likely anyone would even find me, let alone hear of my work . . . Still, it was a wonderful spot to paint in; remotely peaceful with little but the sounds of my subjects to disturb the silence. Ravens, the true rulers of the moorland, tumbled in aerobatic flight over the granite slabs of Crockern Tor, while in the heather red grouse competed with the harsh barking croak of the big black birds with their own territorial warnings, a rattling and peremptory 'G-back, g-back, g-back'. Snipe, lapwing, curlew and plover added their own distinctive cries.

It was – and still is – a heavenly spot. Until winter. The first one was comparatively mild and just about bearable, but it was the second that put paid to any more romantic nonsense about starving artists suffering for their work. There were ten days of bitter numbing wind blowing at gale-force speeds from the Siberian wastes, piling up snow and driving it through every nook and cranny (and there were a great many) of the old farmhouse. Most of the fuel was used up by the second day, and most of the food by the third. Cut off from further supplies, life became a chill and painful routine with most of the time spent lying huddled in bed, fully clothed. Plug gaps in window frames and doorways with newspaper, feed the smouldering lack-lustre fire with a few more precious scraps of kindling – the heat was needed to melt snow for water – swallow a few mouthfuls of cold tinned food and crawl back to bed. Survival. Nothing else. It was impossible to draw or paint with fingers frozen stiff; impossible to do anything except shiver and reflect on the fact that starving for one's art was all very well but freezing for it, too, was no fun at all.

The discomfort of those ten days made me face reality. I had no wish to continue such a hand-to-mouth existence. The moment the snows cleared, I began to look for an additional source of income – and accommodation. Romantic I may have been, but I realized that, in my case, man could not live by paint alone. Pride had little to do with it; wild-life artists are not an uncommon species, particularly in Devon. Clearly, if I was to compete in this market I needed money to find better accommodation, to buy better equipment and materials, and to buy time to practise my craft. Those were my priorities; but there was an additional motive; a very pretty red-head called Anne, whom I was soon to marry.

The accommodation happened first and through a friend I heard of a small cottage for rent near the village of Sampford Spiney. It was not an area I knew well, but the moment I saw the simple granite house I knew it was just what I had been looking for, and I moved in within the week – easel, paints, fishing rods and all.

Sketchbook in hand, I began to investigate my new surroundings. The Walkham valley runs on a north/south axis just to the east of the village surrounded by moorland and marginal grazing, but the real fascination of the upper valley lies in the woodlands. In a comparatively small area one can wander through a complex mosaic of managed and natural plantations that reflect the activities of human beings in a region of poor soil and harsh climate. Close to habitation – or the remains thereof – are the coppices that provided outlying farms with fuel for warmth and cooking, mixed woodland of oak, birch, sycamore, hazel and alder. The majority now stand abandoned, their multi-trunked growths providing a thick canopy under which little can survive.

Surprisingly, for it is really a tree of the chalklands, there are some magnificent stands of beech; the bequest of some caring but forgotten landowner. Many are just past their prime, and it is a sad sight to see their mighty limbs torn to the ground by a winter's gale, or their smooth trunks riven by frost. The attentions of a tree-surgeon would undoubtedly prolong their life, but few, if any, of the upland farmers or landowners have cash to spare, nor, it would appear, has the Dartmoor National Park Authority. It is something of a catch-22, for the majority of these handsome trees are in an area covered by a Tree Preservation Order . . . until the quandary is resolved the beeches will continue to fall, bringing down younger growth, toppling walls and blocking the streams and river. Such windfalls must be cleared and it is a strange anomaly that in an area covered by a preservation order, the most common sound to be heard on a still day is the angry spluttering whine of the chain-saw.

There are a few coniferous plantations, both old and new, which provide a habitat of a different kind where sound is deadened by a thick carpet of pine-needles, and which, in the case of the larch plantations, assume a curiously eerie aspect in the winter, seemingly dead in their leafless condition. Some of the older plantations have long passed maturity and lean precariously over their fallen brethren. Planted around the time of the First World War for future use as pit-props and trench reinforcements, they now stand abandoned, covered in mossy growth for the greater part of their narrow trunks, unthinned and uncared for.

The more open spaces of the upper slopes are home to birch and the mountain ash, or rowan, whose scarlet berries are irresistible to birds who pass the indigestible seeds through their intestines and sow the rowan tree far and wide. Even in the most exposed and inhospitable areas of the moor examples of this hardy little tree are to be found.

I suppose that the term 'natural woodland' must be incorrect, for people have inhabited these lands for so long that it is inconceivable that there can be any part of the valley that has not felt human influence – or perhaps it should be influence-by-proxy, for the greatest changes to the landscape came about not by use of spade, axe or plough, but by the grazing of herbivorous beasts. Their ravages caused the woodland to retreat into the outlying valleys, such as the Walkham, and perhaps it was man himself, seeing the imminent loss of his source of firewood and building materials, who called the halt and began to manage the woods. Perhaps 'ancient woodland' would be a preferable expression; whatever the title, it describes those areas that are more often found in the less accessible parts of the valley: boulder-strewn slopes of hawthorn, holly, and stunted pedunculate oaks so gnarled and twisted that they seem to have been stolen from an Arthur Rackham illustration. Their trunks are often little more than head high, yet some of these trees are incredibly old. I have examined the rings of a fallen tree that was being sawn up and found them impossible to count, partly because of the closeness of the rings, a reflection of the tree's slow growth in such poor surroundings. Mosses and lichen cover the rocks and to a large extent the trees themselves, while ivy wraps itself around the deeply fissured bark.

Through these ancient groves run mysterious underground springs that often appear on the surface from beneath the twisted roots to run down the hillside to join the rushing rocky waters of the Walkham, home to the tiny moorland trout and spawning ground to their larger cousins, the salmon and the peal.

It was fishing that ultimately led to a source of regular income; from the moment that I had moved down to stay with the Clarksons I had begun to explore the local streams and rivers. Fly-fishing was not new to me – it was a technique I had first tried out on chub – but game-fishing, the catching of salmon and trout, was. I

R.A. lands a sea-trout

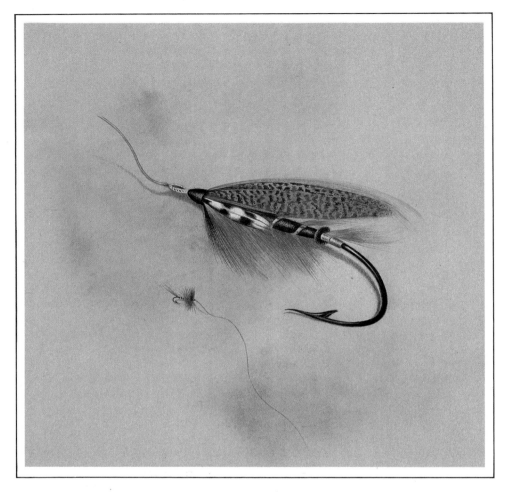

From the sublime to the ridiculous: tiny trout fly as used on our trout streams and
an old gut-eyed salmon fly used in Scotland

became addicted and, when not painting or sketching, I spent long
happy hours trying to master the art beside the rivers and reservoirs of Dartmoor. In doing so I made the acquaintance of a number of river wardens – the official title for the water bailiffs
employed by the South West Water Authority to regulate and
police the fisheries of the area. Always eager for information and
new experience, I often lent them a hand with their more mundane tasks such as clearing fallen branches, inspecting spawning
grounds and counting redds (spawn), and mink-trapping. After a
while I was asked if I would like to become an honorary bailiff –
that is to say, a part-time warden without pay or payment. I
accepted like a shot; the opportunity to walk beside the rivers I was
coming to know and love and to be involved with the care and
maintenance of fish stocks was too good to miss. Eventually, the

position of warden for the Walkham and Tavy rivers fell vacant and I immediately applied.

I became a water bailiff through a combination of good luck, good fortune and good friends – but I suspected that these qualifications were not quite what my friend in Herefordshire had in mind. Experience is the only qualification – but how to gain that experience in the first place? I composed a long and boring letter setting out the steps I thought young James should take; try to get some paper qualifications – English, biology and chemistry being the subjects most useful to a bailiff and likely to impress any future employer – and as far as the art went, to take professional advice. Then I tore it up; practical help is what you need at that age – people had helped me, now it was my turn to do the same. Invite the boy to stay for a week, show him what the job entailed and, if he was still keen, introduce him to an old friend, now a private river-keeper, who was looking for a likely lad. I went to consult my wife.

The snow was falling heavily again and the bitter wind stung my earlobes and reddened my cheeks as I struggled through the drifts. I really didn't see the necessity of posting the letter now when it seemed extremely unlikely that there would be a collection in the next day or so. But Anne had been adamant, pointing out that if I didn't, I'd forget. Just like the car tax and the grocer's bill, she added, pushing the envelopes into my hand. There was just the tiniest hint of steel in her voice – sometimes I wonder whether she has ever forgiven me for putting her on my list of priorities *after* a complete set of extremely expensive sable paintbrushes. Anyway, I made it to the postbox, and wondered if the invitation would ever get through.

Elephant hawk moth

CHAPTER THREE

THE DUE PROCESS

I

A FEW minutes before ten o'clock on a wet Friday, I sheltered under one of the stone arches just across from the entrance to the Magistrates' Court and discussed the forthcoming case with Arthur, chief solicitor for the Water Authority.

'Did you know,' he asked, peering over the top of his spectacles in approved legalistic fashion, 'that Charles I used to make a joke about Tavistock's weather?'

'Oh?'

'Mmm. Apparently he once stayed in the town and ever afterwards, if someone remarked that it was a fine day, he would reply, "But it is undoubtedly raining in Tavistock."'

'Bit of a wet joke . . .'

Arthur gave me an old-fashioned look and returned to his brief. Little more than ten feet away on the other side of the arch stood A, the defendant, and his cronies. Hostility was muted, but they obviously resented our presence as they snickered among themselves and took furtive drags on Marlboro king-size; the rugged range-riding image sat uneasily on narrow shoulders, greasy locks and incipient acne.

Arthur ran through a few points of evidence with me since I was the arresting officer and also chief prosecution witness – somehow such resounding titles seemed unimpressive on such a dismal day. A gust of wind rapped wetly at our trouser legs and I found it increasingly difficult to concentrate on Arthur's legal murmurings. The group opposite laughed uneasily and shuffled their feet. I shared their apprehension; I have never enjoyed appearing in court even though 'my' side is the side of law and order. The policing aspect of being a bailiff is the least enjoyable – although, paradoxically, it can sometimes be the most interesting.

'We can go in now.'

Awoken from my reverie, I followed Arthur and the swaggering defendants across the rainswept carpark to the arched doorway leading to number two court. The Russell family, Dukes of Bedford, built the Guildhall back in 1848 out of profits accruing from the famous Devon Great Consols copper mine. A handsome building, somewhat in the gothic manner, its clean granite façade dominates Bedford Square in the heart of the town, and contains not only the various council offices and chambers but the police station and the two courts.

To my mind it is a particularly attractive and unfussy exercise in Victorian architecture – a solid manifestation of a time of wealth and prosperity. Tavistock has known other such times and has a spirit of sturdy granite-based independence, its shops and houses nestling on the hillsides athwart the river that gives it its name. A centre for the tin-trade – a Stannary town – home to Tavistock Abbey, now just ruins but once an enormously rich and powerful Benedictine establishment whose influence spread far over the West Country, a market-town and a producer of woollen cloth; all these were profitable episodes in the town's past and the copper mines were merely the most recent of the episodes of fortune.

We climbed up the narrow worn stone steps and went into court. The central, or number one, court is rightly impressive. It has a large public seating area, a high raftered roof, a witness box, and a judge's bench resplendent beneath a gilded statue of blind justice surmounted by the royal coat-of-arms, which is, in turn, flanked by the arms of the Prince of Wales and the Russells. Number two court is, however, a different matter. Originally conceived as the judge's robing room, it backs immediately on to the central court and is reached either by the exit doors flanking the judge's bench or by a winding staircase from the carpark. When both courts are in session this can lead to an element of farce if the legal powers-that-be in central court decide to go into recession, since the only way that they can leave is through number two! Number two is merely a moderate-sized room with a large table in the centre. The magistrates sit on one side of this, the clerk at one end, and the defendant and lawyers on the other side. The room itself is warm but airy, with wall-to-wall carpeting and walls the colour of prim-roses. Benches are provided for the various witnesses, family, press, etc., while for those whose presence is legally prohibited during the various stages of proceedings, there is little option but to stand on the narrow landing outside and enjoy the bracing draught gusting up the stair-well.

We followed the magistrates in and remained standing until they were seated. Although I was shortly to be revelling in the delights of the gusty landing, I was permitted to stay and hear the charge read. The solicitors started to lay out their papers while the clerk read out the charge in an unenthusiastic monotone. Surreptitiously I polished my brogues against the backs of my trouser legs. Among the Authority's 'Instructions to River Wardens' is a sentence to the effect that: 'The court's first impression of a Warden is important and to this end a well-dressed Warden is halfway to convincing the bench/jury.' Standing like a heron on one leg, buffing my left toe-cap on my right calf I considered myself to be only a quarter of the way there. Such social niceties, however, didn't seem to bother the accused whose jeans and jersey exhibited the distinguishing marks of his trade as a builder.

Mind you, I'm not sure Arthur looked a lot better with his shirt half out of his trousers and his tweed suit bearing the authentic rumpled look of the country gentleman. During my ill-fated foray into gamekeeping it was said of one of the neighbouring aristo-cratic landowners that he would never wear a suit unless one of his gardeners had worn it for a year or so previously, just to break it in. I doubted whether Arthur had a gardener – let alone several – but it appeared to me that he might have come to an agreement with one of our locally based Royal Marines.

It was time to brave the landing. Rain streaked the mullioned window and a gust of wind rattled the panes. A typical winter's morning on the western edge of Dartmoor. Apart from the fact that it was night-time, the weather was similar some five weeks ago when this particular case started.

II

The public's image of river wardens or water bailiffs is a funny one. We are usually seen in terms of those old *Punch* cartoons drawn by the likes of Du Maurier or Ravenhill.

Scene: a well-manicured river bank bristling with 'Private Fishing' notices. A bored-looking ragamuffin is fishing with stick, string, bent pin and worm. It is evident that he has had little success. He is confronted by a pompous-looking individual (the bailiff) wielding a stout stick.

BAILIFF: 'Oi, you can't fish 'ere.'

RAGAMUFFIN (morosely): ''Oo's fishin'?'

As they used to say: Collapse of Stout Party.

True, we do patrol the river banks checking that licences and permits are in order during the season, and that fish are being

Hole in the wall in Autumn

caught by legal methods as defined in the Salmon and Freshwater Fisheries Act 1975 and the various Water Authority bye-laws. However, we are also concerned with the maintenance of fish stocks, pollution, river engineering, vermin control, prevention of poaching, and the endless stream of paperwork that all this diligent grafting produces. In this part of the world we are, in fact, called river wardens as opposed to water bailiffs and since my old Oxford Dictionary defines the former as 'a guardian' and the latter as 'an agent' I reckon that's a pretty fair summation, for bailiffs tend to be in private employ and responsible for a comparatively short stretch of water, while wardens look after the river as a whole and have far greater legal authority and power of arrest under the aforementioned Fisheries Act.

Mind you, all that was very far from my mind on that late October night five weeks ago. Young Owen had been put to bed, tired out by the endless busy fascinations of a two-year-old's world, and my wife was having a bath. As the prevailing south-westerly gusted up the Walkham valley it made the fire smoke slightly and I closed the vent a fraction and returned to polishing the latest addition to my reel collection. A 1923 2¼-inch nickel-plated fly-reel by Hardy Brothers, the Purdeys of the fishing world. I remember feeling smugly satisfied. I had swapped a small painting for the reel earlier that evening, while the day had been spent clearing a fallen tree from a small but valuable spawning ground – hard, wet work, but immensely satisfying. A profitable day all round and made doubly so by the sighting of an otter's pug-mark on a crumbling section of bank immediately upstream from the fallen spruce. Since it was well protected by the broad shiny leaves of a rhododendron I had hopes that it might still be there by morning, in which case I would make a cast of it.

The telephone rang.

The pips of a coin-box were followed by the sound of breathing and a background murmur of voices and clinking sounds.

'If you want to catch A, B, and the C brothers, they're just off down to Grenofen.'

The phone went dead. I noted down the time and thought for a moment. He was obviously speaking from a pub but I didn't recognize his voice. Like the police we get a lot of anonymous tip-offs; sometimes a public-spirited citizen who just doesn't want to be involved, but more often somebody with a grudge – often a fellow-poacher. Whoever it is, it's information one cannot afford to ignore, particularly at a time when the salmon and peal are venturing up rivers swollen by autumnal rain.

Dave was the duty warden that night so I rang him. Having alerted the police, I grabbed a hat and jacket, shouted a farewell at the bathroom door and set off in the car in the direction of Grenofen bridge where we had arranged to meet.

So much for reels, paw-prints of otters and paintings. I checked my VHF radio, warrant-card, notebook, torch and ballpoint. Spare waterproofs and boots were in the back together with plastic bags for any evidence found. Handcuffs and a whistle were in my trouser pocket. Romance flies out of the window when reality intrudes.

Cover as many miles of river as we do and the technology of the twentieth century certainly has its uses. Without modern transport and communications the thirty or so wardens in the employ of the Water Authority would be helpless to protect more than one river.

The whole region had been drought-stricken during the summer and everyone was desperate for the clouds to empty – but I could have done without the rain that night. It began to pelt down as I turned off the road and down the track to where A, B and the C brothers – old adversaries – were reputedly at work.

III

It was still raining five weeks later as I sat at the back of number two court, but at least the rain was outside and merely lent a sheen to the high arched windows. It was easy to forget that the cosy room with its homely trappings was a court of law. The magistrates'

Plaster cast of the otterprint I took at Buckland Water

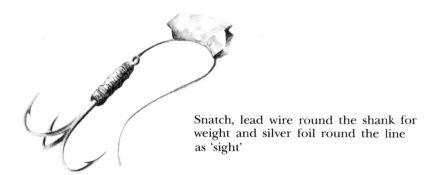

Snatch, lead wire round the shank for weight and silver foil round the line as 'sight'

coats hung on a stand under the window and beside these unremarkable garments were two ancient safes, their once bright enamel chipped and dull. I wondered what they contained. Probably the clerk of the court's thermos and sandwiches.

'A "snatch", Your Worship, is a large hook or hooks which can be cast over the stationary fish and reeled in rapidly in such a manner as to enable the barbs of the hooks to sink into the flesh.'

Arthur was trying to make things clear to a newcomer to the bench – evidently not a fishing man. The other two were old hands at the game and probably knew as much as, if not more than, I did about the various techniques and gadgets beloved of the poaching fraternity.

'I see,' said His Worship. Judging by the expression on his face, he didn't.

It was easy to understand his bewilderment. After all, plenty of people catch fish, don't they? Well, yes, but these men hadn't done it by 'sporting means', for the essential difference between fishing and all other forms of sport is that the hunter allows his quarry the freedom of choice; it is up to the fish whether it takes the bait or not. Slinging a bunch of hooks big enough to satisfy the most prudent of shark-fishermen over the back of a five-pound sea trout or peal (as happened in this case) and 'snatching' it deep into its flanks as it swims stationary with the current can hardly be said to be giving the fish freedom of choice in the matter of its demise.

The defence lawyer, a smart young solicitor from Plymouth, called Mr B. No great court-room ceremony here, no clerks, constables and ushers to bring witnesses in from some oak-panelled ante-room. Getting the nod from the chairman, the solicitor took four paces to the door and brought in young B from the narrow landing – the clerk being busy with his notes. Strangely, this lack of formality often produces good results since witnesses are less overawed by their surroundings and are generally prepared to be more forthcoming.

We were getting to the nub of the case. 'Acting on information received' as the ponderous jargon has it, Dave and I had met up in the carpark at Grenofen bridge 'on the night in question'. There was no sign of anybody, even after two hours of searching up and down the bank, struggling through bramble and fern and getting soaked. On an off-chance, Dave went to the next bridge upstream, Magpie, and reported back that there was a car in the small car-park. One o'clock in the morning of a wet and windy moonless night on the western fringes of Dartmoor is hardly the time of day to park your car and go sightseeing.

Having transmitted the car's number through to the police, we sat down to wait in the undergrowth at the entrance to the Magpie bridge carpark. After an hour, the only diversion from our discomfort was provided by the arrival on foot of two constables who had heard of our problems over their car radio and, deciding that a breath of fresh air would be welcome after the fug of their Granada, had parked their patrol car at the top of the lane and wandered down to see if they could be of assistance.

We invited the two stalwart constables to share our wet and spiky refuge. This appealed enormously to the elder of the pair once he realized that a large proportion of the thicket was composed of blackthorn. He produced a large plastic carrier bag from somewhere on his person and promptly began harvesting the immediate sloe-crop. Since the sole illumination for this activity came from intermittent gleams of moonlight through the low scudding clouds, the gathering was accompanied by muttered curses, as his fingers caught on the long hardwood thorns.

Dave's interest was aroused. 'Spot o' gin?'

The affirmative touched off a murmured exchange of recipes for sloe-gin and a mutual interest in home-brewing, while the younger policeman shivered beside me and tried to see into the gloom beyond the black bulk of the suspect car.

''Course, these young sloes're real sharp. I reckon you'll need less'n a pound to a pint and a half of gin . . . '

' . . . Always add a dash of almond essence meself . . . '

The conversation suddenly died away. Nothing could be heard above the sound of the wind in the tree-tops but shadowy movement could be discerned by the abandoned car. Ideally, I would like to say that at this point we left our cover silently with consummate woodcraft and leapt on the suspects with an athletic spring; but, as usual, the truth was rather more mundane. First, it is impossible to move silently when wearing waterproof clothing that is firmly gripped by bramble and thorn and, second, two hours sitting in a crouched huddle exposed to the elements on a winter's night does little to promote suppleness and athleticism. It was with an arthritic lurch, accompanied by ripping and tearing sounds, that I stumbled towards the car, switching on my torch as I did so.

The tableau round the driver's door of the car froze momentarily. Whoever the anonymous caller was, and whatever his motive, there was no doubting the veracity of his information. A, B and the brothers C were caught in the uncertain beam – A with a shepherd's lambing torch, B with a fishing rod and a plastic bag, and the two brothers carrying, respectively, a garden fork and a short stick. Instant Poachers – just add water. Then they ran. The two brothers and B made for the track leading out of the carpark and A doubled back towards the river. With an incoherent yell I dashed after A, only to measure my length on the tarmac after about six paces. From this commanding position I shouted after the dwindling figure: 'Stop! I am a water bailiff and want to search you.'

Since most of the wind had been knocked out of me by the fall it sounded less than convincing. A obviously thought so, for he vanished completely. Grazed of palm and shorn of dignity I limped off in the direction of the track where confused shouting seemed to indicate that my companions had had more luck.

Three wet and miserable poachers stood illuminated in the torch light, framed by one equally wet but no-longer-miserable officer of the law and Dave, the younger constable having been sent back to collect the patrol car and radio in for additional transport. Once the unhappy trio had been cautioned and placed in the back of the Granada in company with the driver, we started a search for A and the evidence abandoned in their flight up the track. The snare-

Licensed netsmen at work

stick, fork, fishing rod with snatch, and the plastic bag containing four small peal were found almost immediately, but of their companion-in-arms and his powerful lamp there was no sign. The piles of wet beech and oak leaves blew back and forth over the track, and some sheep, disturbed from their shelter, trampled out any footprints there might have been as they skittered on the greasy mud.

A false dawn was breaking by the time we gave up the search and wearily made our way back to our own abandoned vehicles.

IV

'. . . The truth, the whole truth, andnothingbutthetruthsohelpmeGodamen.'

Bit of a rush at the end. Steady up and remember the points detailed in the Authority's Notes on Court Appearances. Read the oath from the card rather than gabble it out in a bored monotone, stand up straight and address the bench, and whatever you do don't put your hands in your pockets. Remember the instruction that 'whilst there is considerable goodwill from benches towards Wardens there is a need to be more professional and polished in our approach without losing the desirable image of dedicated country gentlemen for whom poacher-catching is not the only thing in life.' A country gentleman? One thing's for certain, poacher-catching is very far from being the only thing in my life – physical discomfort, lack of sleep and the distinct possibility of being thumped one dark night are hardly experiences to be cherished. Besides, in this particular case, the expression is something of a misnomer since we didn't exactly catch the accused. His three companions were dealt with in court a fortnight ago but when I eventually ran A to ground in his mother's council house the following day he strenuously denied being anywhere near the river that night. This was somewhat at odds with the statements made at the police station by the other three who all incriminated him, statements that were to be radically altered by the time they appeared in court. Yes, said B and the brothers C, they were guilty of offences under the Salmon and Freshwater Fisheries Act 1975 (i.e. poaching) and they were very sorry and wouldn't do it again, but no, Mr A was definitely not with them on the night in question. Hence this second trial.

Arthur was on his feet, facing me. 'Will you tell the bench, in your own words, what happened after you discovered the motorcar at, um, Magpie bridge.'

With my notebook open at the relevant, rain-stained page I began. The accused slumped in his chair staring vacantly into space as his solicitor frowned at his notes, the clerk scribbled away industriously, and the magistrates took judicial interest in proceedings. On a side bench, a member of the public dozed quietly beside the industrious young lady representative of the press, who busied herself with Pitman and pencil.

' . . . We switched on our torches, and in the light I saw A, B and the brothers C.'

'Crap.'

If number two court didn't have wall-to-wall carpets you could have heard the proverbial pin drop; even the somnolent member of the public woke up. In these liberal times bad language is not unknown in courts – but it normally comes in the form of reported speech from the witness stand. The shock created by this interjection was not so much because of the word, but because it was not A's turn to speak. For an instant the scene was reminiscent of one of those splendid H. M. Bateman cartoons: the chairman of the bench raised one of her immaculately plucked eyebrows a millimetre and looked not at the accused but at his solicitor. Reddening, he turned to his client (The Man Who Swore In Court) and admonished him in a hoarse whisper while everybody else gazed with sudden interest at notes, ceiling or wall. The whispering over, A slumped lower in his chair and scowled ferociously at the table.

Arthur cleared his throat, rustled his notes, and started again.

'You positively identified the accused?'

'I did.'

'And how long have you known him?'

'Nine years.'

'Nine years. Um, well, thank you, Mr Armstrong.'

Arthur sat down and the nattily-dressed defence rose, did a bit of theatrical business with glasses and notes, grasped his lapel with right hand in approved lawyerly fashion, cleared his throat and frowned.

'Mr Armstrong, on the night in question it was raining heavily, was it not?'

'Yes.'

'And in your statement to the court, you said that you caught the suspects at two-thirty in the morning?'

'Yes.'

'And you also said that there was considerable confusion at the time?'

'Yes.'

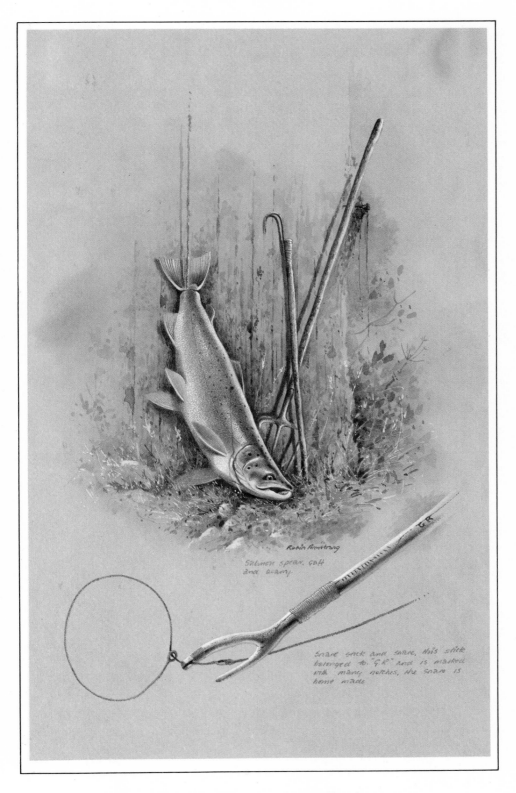

The poacher's hoard: salmon spear, gaff and quarry

'And yet you positively identified the accused, Mr A, in the course of all this confusion, and on a dark and rainy night?'

'Yes.'

'Thank you, Mr Armstrong. With Your Worship's permission, I should like to ask Mr B to stand at the back of the court.'

The clerk went over to the door and brought B off the landing. He stood by the dozing spectator and shifted from foot to foot uneasily.

'Mr A, will you please stand.'

A got sulkily to his feet.

'Mr Armstrong, I put it to you that in the muddle and poor visibility in the carpark you were mistaken as to the number of suspects present, and that you also mistook Mr B for Mr A. Your Worships will note the similarity . . . '

A real Perry Mason, this one. True, there was no resemblance in height, build, colouring or dress; but they did both have straggling moustaches.

'No.'

'Perry' didn't seem at all put out and sat down with a self-satisfied expression. B was ushered out to the joyless comforts of the stair-well and Arthur rose to remind the bench, through me, about the length of time I had been acquainted with the accused. Having made his point, I was dismissed and allowed to sit on the form against the wall. The rain seemed to be easing and I didn't know whether to be sad or sorry; fine weather could mean that the pug-mark would still be intact so that I could place a cardboard wall round it, pour in plaster of paris and make a really good cast – on the other hand, we needed every inch of rain we could get to fill the parched reservoirs and raise the level of the rivers to get the fish to their spawning beds. It's obvious which was the more important, but selfishly I couldn't help hoping the rain would just hold off for a few more hours.

One of the C brothers was cross-questioned as to why he changed his original statement. Ill at ease before the magistrates, he replied in a thick mumble. The gist of the story appeared to be that he was cold, wet and tired and wanted to go home and get a change of clothes, but, because he had agreed to make a statement, the police would not let him go until he had. Under further pressure from Perry Mason it transpired that the brutal river warden had told him that if he wanted to go home and change that year, then he had better implicate the innocent A, because he, the BRW, was 'out to get A'.

This was getting good – corruption and brutality, public official accused. The young lady from the local paper was scribbling like fury – much more and she'd need another notebook. It was becoming difficult to remember that the whole affair was over four little fish, three of them barely over two pounds in weight. Their silvery cadavers lay in the Water Authority's freezer, wrapped in a plastic bag and tagged with the reference number of this particular case. Three of them had been taken with a snatch, and the fourth and largest tailed out with a noose or snare attached to the end of a stick.

C had finished giving evidence and sat down on the same bench as myself, wiping his hands with a faded spotted handkerchief. Arthur was looking slightly worried and was preparing to question the amazing look-alike, Mr B. I wondered what I could possibly have threatened him with – flogging or the rack? I needn't have worried. B had an entirely different story to tell. It would appear that he and the defendant had had 'a bit of a ding-dong, loike', and that he had a grudge against A, and when given the opportunity to incriminate him by means of a false statement had done so. No mention of intimidating behaviour on the part of bent bailiffs and the like.

'So involving Mr A by means of a false statement was entirely your idea?'

'S'right.'

'And you persuaded your accomplices to aid and abet you with this farrago of lies?'

'Beg pardon?'

'You, ah, persuaded the C brothers to tell the same story as yourself?'

'Yer.'

'Why?'

Otter mask

'Well, Oi thought Oi'd troi an' stitch 'im up, loike.'

Five weeks and the added bonus of standing together for some fifty minutes on the courtroom landing and they still couldn't get their yarns to tally.

Arthur took great pleasure in pointing out these discrepancies to the court, while the defence solicitor in his summing up wisely steered clear of such matters and merely returned to suggesting that I may have been mistaken in the matter of identification in the carpark mêlée.

The magistrates withdrew to consider the case, disappearing up the stairs in the direction of some mysterious attic room. We humbler beings remained standing after they had left and gathered in two groups on either side of the table, poachers nearest the window. The clerk of the court was not all that optimistic. It always worries me when it seems as if we're going to lose a case; the waste of all that time and trouble, the endless paperwork, the serving of summons, the time away from work. Besides, I always get a bad attack of the collywobbles before speaking in public – it doesn't matter if it's a talk to the Whitchurch Womens' Institute on the life-cycle of the salmon or a court appearance. Finally, there is an added worry: as the arresting warden and case officer, did I do everything right according to the rules and regulations?

The clerk put his head round the door and muttered,' They're coming back,' then louder, 'Court will rise.'

We stood and waited for their Worships' verdict.

V

Sunday evening; a dark November night with a hint of frost in the clear still air, but inside the cottage all was snug. Anne and a fellow-schoolteacher were sitting on the sofa discussing the events of their day and my son and daughter were tucked up in bed, asleep.

I examined the contents of the box balanced on my knee. The plaster cast had come out well – a left fore-paw with its broad webbed imprint standing well clear. Once a common sight around the moorland streams and rivers, the otter has sadly become something of a rarity; I have seen only four individuals since I moved here, although I have found traces of many more. Their decline in these parts would seem to have less to do with hunting, pollution or water-abstraction than with the activities of that alien intruder to the moor, the mink. Most experienced local anglers and natural-

A brown trout nearly beaten comes to the net

ists seem to agree on this point, since the number of otters declined significantly in the late 1950s – not long after the mink first made their appearance.

I looked at the cast again. An adult, probably just resting for a moment or two in the shelter of the rhododendrons before engaging in a similar activity to A, B and the brothers C – the thought of whom sowed a small seed of concern in my mind. I crossed over to the window and pulled back the curtain. It was a beautiful night, crystal clear and as crisp as a cos, the sky resembling a black velvet tent hung with minute diamonds. I decided to wrap up warmly, thermal underwear, two pairs of socks, balaclava – the lot. It was going to be a cold night down by the river.

You see, while I had been waiting for the plaster to harden, and had been consequently sitting *very* still in the middle of my rhododendron bush, A had come by on the footpath on the other side of the stream, stopping every so often and looking intently into the various pools. So what, you might ask. Well, for a start there's nothing wrong with his eyesight and he had been wearing dark glasses on a November afternoon – almost certainly polaroids which cut out the reflections of the water and enable an out-of-season fish to be spotted easily.

It's a free country, you might reply, and he had been on the public right-of-way. True, but then I'm a nasty suspicious river warden, and anyway, if you were a poacher who had just been fined a total of £150 at Tavistock Magistrates' Court, where would you go to get the money?

CHAPTER FOUR

FROM DUNS TO DIGESTIVES

I

Written Report Writing. Written communication is a skill which must be practised . . . Wardens' Weekly Reports pass information from the 'field' to the 'office'. They are the first step in the reporting chain. They are also an important record which is always available for future use. They should be sent to the head warden by Tuesday of the following week.

from 'WEEKLY REPORT WRITING',
SWWA trainee handout

IF there's one thing I hate, it's writing to order. As a child I was always getting into trouble for not writing thank-you letters at Christmas or on birthdays, and matters haven't improved greatly with age. Filling in forms and writing reports are, as far as I am concerned, one of the very few unpleasant aspects of my job; one that I am prepared to go to almost any lengths to postpone. If I devote a Sunday morning to report-writing then undoubtedly I shall be suffering from severe tannin poisoning by lunchtime because, while most people will pause for elevenses, I will stop at any pretext and make tea at nineses, tenses and twelveses as well. I drive my wife scatty by starting – but not finishing – odd jobs around the house or garden; half-painted walls and well-manured holes abound.

This particular Sunday the excuse was provided by the finicky art of fly-tying; although I doubt that the hairy little botched-up creations that I produce can be classified as art. I have been privileged to know and watch some of the country's finest fly-tiers, both amateur and professional, and for all their kind words of advice I still cannot produce anything like the delicate and entrancing little

imitations that come from their skilled fingers. Like most people with some artistic ability, I am a perfectionist and know in my mind's eye exactly how the finished product should look; inevitably, the results are nearly always disappointing. However, I had developed a theory that perhaps I was trying too hard and that a more relaxed approach might yield better results. As a self-taught water-colourist, I have often found that this approach yields the more interesting results so it seemed worth a try. Naturally, all this theorizing conveniently delayed completion of my weekly report . . .

Into the beak of the tying-vice went a no. 14 hook, and out came the old black cash-box in which I keep oddments of fur and feather. The first fly I ever attempted was that useful little classic, the Olive Dun; it was also, because of sheer ignorance, the only one I have ever been really pleased with! That was well over twenty years ago and I remember every step in the process of its construction as if it were yesterday. I had no patent vice, so I 'borrowed' a pair of pliers from my father's tool-kit and wrapped a couple of thick rubber bands round the grips to keep the jaws closed. This device was then crudely lashed to the back of a kitchen chair and the rest of the tools comprised tweezers and a razor-blade, plus a small, plastic, magnifying glass that had come out of a Christmas cracker. Materials required a greater degree of ingenuity; the formula for tying an Olive Dun calls for 'dyed medium olive seal's fur for the body, starling's wing feather for wings, olive cock's hackle, and tail three whisks as per hackle'. Now in 1960, the St Paul's Cray area of south London was singularly lacking in such exotic substances with the honourable exception of starlings. Two blood-marbles and a copy of *Hotspur* secured the loan of an air-rifle and led to the subsequent demise of a *Sternus vulgaris* that unwittingly perched on the back-garden fence. The other materials required substitutes which were provided, in the case of the seal, by next-door's mangy mongrel bitch, and in the case of the cock's hackle, by a raid on a neighbour-

Brimstone butterfly

Robin Armstrong

to Anne, on the birth
of our son Owen, love.
A.

Singing starling

ing bird-fancier's cage. Total cost: two marbles, a comic and a dog-bite. The fact that I did not have the equipment, the means or the opportunity to try out the resulting creation on an unwary trout was of little consequence.

All these years later, and armed with the correct equipment and materials, I decided to try again. As I wound waxed silk on to the shank of the hook, I reflected on my changed circumstances and felt quietly satisfied with my good fortune; from a sprawling council estate in London to an old cottage on the wooded slopes of the Walkham valley of western Dartmoor is a change I never have regretted – even if the price to be paid involves the writing of reports . . .

I tied in three hackle-whisks for the tail, and slipped a couple of half-hitches underneath it to give it a jaunty lift. So far, so good. I admired my handiwork, while my conscience reflected on the weekly report. The water in the two rivers that comprise my 'patch' was alarmingly low for the time of year. The Tavy and the Walkham are probably two of the fastest rivers in the whole of England, yet for several weeks now they had been moving with all the pace of a thoughtful snail. Lack of rain was forcing the vast natural sponge of the moor to release its waters grudgingly. The river that runs some two hundred yards from my cottage was reduced to little more than a series of small clear streams connecting the boulder-lined pools rather than the rushing torrent of peaty-brown water that is the norm for this time of the year. Quite naturally, this lack of rain was causing more than a little·concern to my employers, to whom the word 'drought' is anathema. They are in the invidious position of always being in the wrong as far as public opinion is concerned; a lack of water and they are accused of 'short-sightedness in the planning department', yet if they offer to construct a reservoir the outcry is 'desecration of the landscape'. Obviously there can be no simple solution, although it is worth remembering that as long as people have inhabited the moor they have exploited the waters that run off it by damming or diversion, whether for domestic or industrial use. Leats, little canal-like ditches, criss-cross large areas of the land carrying water, the most famous of these being Drake's Leat, built under the supervision of the great Sir Francis, Tavistock's most famous son, which runs seventeen miles from Meavy carrying water to Plymouth and which was completed in 1591.

The popular view of the South West is usually coloured by such images as the palms and beaches of Torquay, or by the Cornish Riviera, or by sleepy little thatched hamlets nestling among rolling combes. It is the prevailing south-westerly airstream which provides the mild, if slightly damp, climate so familiar to holiday-makers. Dartmoor, however, is rather a different kettle of fish, being the greatest natural watershed in the South West. With the highest summits reaching over two thousand feet, the rain-bearing clouds wafted in from the Atlantic are naturally encouraged to shed their load on the moor. At Princetown, less than four miles from where I live, the average annual rainfall is well over eighty inches! As a farmer friend of mine from that area put it: 'Sometimes it do seem that everything fall on Oi.' Not surprising when you consider that snow in April is not uncommon on his high grazing. This year, though, things were looking very different; that same farmer could be heard muttering about the good prospects of 'some proper hay-makin' weather at last'. I am a great believer in listening to local weather-lore, particularly if it comes from a farmer or a fisherman, whose livelihood is so closely concerned with its vagaries. Not for them intensive analysis of barometric pressure, or the recitation of quaint little jingles, but merely an instinctive awareness of natural phenomena, absorbed through generations of experience and observation. Of course, they take notice of the meteorologists' advice, but they temper it with their own knowledge gained through the feeling of the wind on a cheek, the patterns of the clouds, and the behaviour of animals and plants.

Lack of rain is a great problem as far as we river wardens are concerned, for our responsibility is with the game fish of the streams and rivers of the South West, and an insufficient flow of water poses a severe threat to their existence, particularly in rivers such as the Tavy and Walkham, since their very steepness requires a healthy flow of water to enable salmon and sea trout to ascend to the upper reaches in order to spawn. It is interesting to compare these two rivers with the Tamar with which the Tavy shares a common estuary. The longer and larger Tamar is comparatively slow-moving and has an average fall of less than one-sixth of that of the Tavy and its tributary, the Walkham. The Tamar moves ponderously through a great deal of low-lying agricultural land with its attend-ant rich soil, which, in turn, promotes weed growth and a rich var-iety of plant and insect life; ideal for the native brown trout, but of little interest to those nomads from the sea, the salmon and the sea trout or peal. They delight in fast-flowing, highly oxygenated waters, with stretches of gravel bed in which to spawn, and they have scant concern for the degree of food available. A reduced flow in such rivers results in fish being stranded in the lower pools, prey to the poacher, man or beast, and subject to starvation, parasitism and disease. It is possible to capture some of these fish, strip them of their milt (soft roe) and eggs and rear the parr (young) artificially for eventual release into the headwaters of the river of origin; it is a technique we use frequently to conserve stocks, particularly where there has been a disaster such as pollution or disease. None of this, however, will help the embryo fish already in our rivers; alevin, parr and fry will be at the mercy of every predator in the river for the food supply in the acid highland water is poor even when the river is high. Lowering the water also exposes thousands of the newly deposited and fertilized eggs to the air.

As far as the fish are concerned, the level of water in the river is analogous to the level of mercury in a barometer: when high the prospect is fine, but 'ware trouble when low.

II

In real life the barometer was high and the weather reflected the fact, with little cloud, spring sunshine and a dry cool breeze from the east. I set the fly aside (the initial good start being somewhat spoiled by a hackle akin to an Elizabethan ruff) and gazed out of the window. No sign of rain in the sky whose only visible occupant was a buzzard wheeling smoothly overhead mewing plaintively to its unseen mate somewhere beyond the tree-line. As a final act of procrastination I decided to check the trap set beside the river

Stunted oak

bank below Woodtown and then take the car and check a few likely pools further downstream before writing the report.

Poachers fill into two categories – four-legged and two-legged; the trap was set for one of the former – mink. Man rid Dartmoor of the pine-marten and the pole-cat but thoughtlessly replaced them with a far more destructive member of the same family. The North American mink was first introduced into this country in the 1920s to supply the demand for fur. Unfortunately, the financial returns were not as healthy as had been hoped, and with the collapse of a number of businesses, and the subsequent escape or release of live-stock, the mink began to colonize the countryside. The first colony in this part of the world was reported on the Teign in the late fifties; since that time they have spread at an alarming rate. If man himself is public enemy number one to the river environment because of water abstraction and pollution, then, in my opinion, the mink must be number two. This view is naturally coloured by the opinions of others who have spent most of their lives beside the rivers and streams of Devon, but even in the seventeen years I have lived here the depredations of the mink have been alarmingly noticeable. When the Walkham first became part of my beat, kingfishers and dippers, those two most attractive of riverside birds, were common in the wooded reaches. Within a few years, their numbers have declined significantly, and since farming activity is low in the area and the woodland reaches remain to a large extent unspoiled by man, the culprit can be none other than the mink.

An adult mink can grow to over two feet in length and weigh as much as four pounds and is an utterly ruthless predator, as any fish- or chicken-farmer will bear witness. Worse, to my mind, is the destruction the mink causes among the natural inhabitants of the river and its banks. Since mink can climb as well as they can swim, little is safe from their jaws.

The two that had been sighted were less than a mile from my cottage, so I had set a spring-cage trap in a bramble thicket in the vicinity, baited with cat food. The first sighting had come from a local angler of immense experience, if of a somewhat military temper ('Dam' thing just sat on the bloody bank glaring at me. About time you fellows got off your backsides and did something'). That complaint had been delivered at the beginning of the week and the offender in question had been described as 'a big brown bugger', which told me that there were at least two mink in the area for I had seen one myself while scouting around for a suitable site for the trap.

Shortly before dusk on Monday evening I had been standing in

Grey mink seen at Sprys Ham, dragging a large eel. The mink finally dragged the
eel over the bank and I could see bite marks all around its head

the lee of a large rhododendron bush watching the opposite bank
for signs of my quarry, when I became aware of a commotion on
my side of the Walkham, just upstream from where I stood. Now
the river at that point levels out from its initial steep rush off the
moor and widens out into a series of gravel-bedded pools – favourite spawning grounds for the spring and late summer salmon.
These shallows are also attractive to domestic animals and the
sheep and cattle have worn deep tracks along the river bank where
they have come to drink. It was one on one of these paths, covered
with dry dead leaves disturbed by the easterly winds, that the rum-
pus was taking place. A rustling, followed by a thud, followed by a
great deal more rustling. Into view came an extraordinary sight – a
mink and a large eel locked together in a sinuous and deadly
struggle. The eel was well over a foot longer than the mink and was

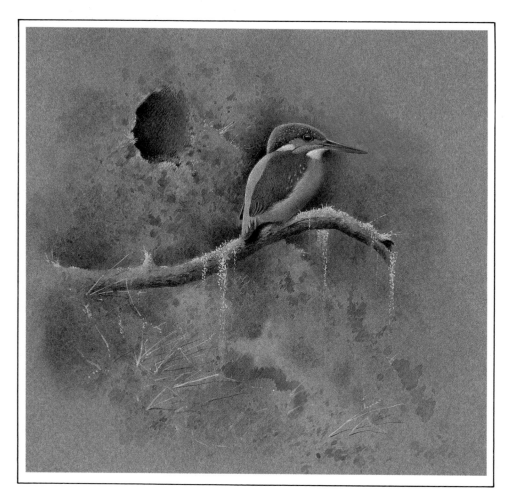

Kingfisher and nest site, Buckland Water

coiled around its body. The mink struggled convulsively to free itself. It was of a colour I had never seen before; no 'brown bugger' this, for its coat was almost silver in sheen, a delicate smoky grey. Its jaws were firmly fastened into the eel's body some three inches below the neck, and as the two animals squirmed together on the path, the mink, whenever it found itself the right way up, would heave itself and its prey forward with a spasmodic leap to land with a thump and begin battle over again. Nearer and nearer the two antagonists came, apparently taking no notice of my presence. At a spot where cattle had crumbled the bank underfoot, the water had washed the soil away to expose a bunch of roots, and with a massive effort the mink dragged the eel towards a hole amid this tangle. I remained, fascinated, as they vanished from sight some five feet from where I stood. I was just about to investigate the hole when, to my amazement, the eel reappeared head-first, and slithered over the gravel to the safety of the water where it swam rapidly downstream, appearing little handicapped by the gaping wound in its neck. Although I waited, the silvery mink did not come out in pursuit and I assumed it was exhausted by the long struggle.

I had set the spring-cage trap close to the hole in the roots, but although I had visited it every morning and evening that week there had been no occupant. Either the mink had decided to turn their noses up at the bait or, more likely, they sensed the trap. With a dollop of fresh temptation in a plastic bag I set off for the river.

III

Spring-cage traps are humane in that they capture the animal intact. The bait is set at the far end of the cage, the unsuspecting animal enters in search of the free meal, and its weight unlatches a powerful spring-loaded door which slams shut behind it. It is, of course, necessary to visit the trap at regular intervals to ensure that the animal does not starve to death or that it does not contain a perfectly innocent member of the animal world. Trying to get an irate tabby with a fondness for Kit-E-Kat out of a cage that is patently too small for him is no easy matter! We are sometimes asked why we do not use more ruthless methods against an adversary as bloodthirsty and as alien to our environment as the mink– methods such as the snare, the fen-trap, poisoning bait, or even gassing. The answer lies in our job-description; we are river wardens employed by the Regional Water Authority and, as such, have a responsibility for policing all the rivers that come under that authority. Since there are only 35 full-time wardens to cover 560 miles of rivers (ignoring the land and sea that we also cover) it can be seen that we are spread pretty thinly on the ground – something like 16 miles of river per warden. With such a large area to cover, it would be impossible to use such devices with any degree of discrimination; assuming, of course, that the riparian owners in question would give their permission, an unlikely event when one considers the numbers of domestic pets and children who would be at risk. For the privately employed river-keeper or water bailiff it is naturally a different matter – the proper use of such traps requires skill and a detailed knowledge of the local environment and, above all, constant supervision; Authority wardens simply do not have time to fulfil these demands. Hence the employment of the large and bulky spring-cage trap, and on a limited scale only.

That afternoon the spring-cage trap demonstrated the proper qualities of selectivity and humaneness that earns it the seal of approval from the Ministry of Agriculture and Fisheries, for when I pushed into the brambles to retrieve it I discovered it contained the long-awaited customer – a large brown dog-mink who spat and chittered with rage as I eased the wire cage from under the thorns.

It is a sad fact of life that the countryside is not full of those lovable little furry creatures that populate so much of our childhood literature – and there is nothing like being confronted by a large mink in a murderous frenzy to drive that fact home. The next point to consider is, what do you do with your mink once you've caught it? The official line is not very helpful, for it advises dispatching the beast by means of a .22 bullet, presumably while it is still in the trap. I do not possess such a weapon, nor do I intend going through the necessary rigmarole to get one just for the purpose of shooting caged mink. True, I do own a shotgun, but that would be a singularly messy – not to say expensive – solution since the cage would certainly go west with the mink.

The first time I caught a mink there was nobody around to advise me. Faced by a fury with teeth in a galvanized wire cage, I tentatively poked at it with my twelve-bladed Swiss Army penknife – but the blade was too short. I considered driving the animal some miles distant and releasing it – but then it would just go on slaughtering on someone else's patch. If I opened the cage door fast enough I might be able to crush it with a stone – but the speed at which it whipped around within the cage decided me against that plan. Eventually, I lugged the trap and its occupant the mile and a half back to the house, got out a plastic fertilizer sack and, with a nasty bite on the fleshy part of the palm, inveigled the mink into the sack. Now came the 'humane' part; I started up the car and clamped the mouth of the sack over the exhaust pipe. The frantic scrabbling and squeaking seemed to go on for ever and my head was reeling with fumes by the time the pitiful struggle ended. A mild case of carbon monoxide poisoning and yet another bite were the net results – for the mink had bitten neatly through the bag and escaped.

This time I was less squeamish. I simply tied a line to the trap and threw it into a deep pool . . .

After a few minutes, I recovered it, threw the limp and sodden body well away, and re-set and re-baited the trap. There was, after all, the matter of the little silver-furred felon to be settled.

IV

On the way to check the likely salmon-lies before surrendering to the inevitable and putting pen to paper, I called in at the Newt's place. Devonians are a great people for nicknames; among the poaching fraternity we have the likes of the said Newt, plus others such as Brummie, Sniffer, Janner, Spud, Gobbler and the Hulk, while on the side of law and order are to be found Mouse, James Pond, Whiskers and GodFrog – the last-named being in charge of the Devon and Cornwall Police Underwater Search Unit! It came as quite a shock to discover in the solemnity of the Magistrates' Court that these colourful personages had perfectly ordinary names like the rest of us.

The Newt is a particular favourite of mine – stocky, burly, in his early forties but definitely one of the lads, he is unusual for a local poacher in that he is a moderately successful local businessman. The majority of our local offenders are casual labourers, redundant or unemployed, but the Newt runs a small contracting business with a side-line in second-hand agricultural machinery; he poaches fish not for any particular monetary gain, but merely, as he freely admits, 'for the sport of it, like'. Fellow-wardens have told me that he was a holy terror on the rivers in his youth and a familiar figure in the courts, but maturity and financial security have made him wary and it is over two years since he last felt a warden's hand on his shoulder. He has his own highly developed, if somewhat idiosyncratic, morality when it comes to taking fish illegally, and for that reason is always worth a visit since he disapproves of many of his contemporaries, particularly those gangs which strip whole sections of the river of fish, and he is not above tipping us the wink.

It was not for this reason, though, that I decided to visit him at his home: I went out of curiosity, for one of his neighbours, a man not entirely above suspicion where such activities are concerned, had reported that there was a net hanging up to dry in the Newt's garden. A case of the grass grassed on? What was unusual was that the Newt had never been known as a netsman, preferring to take his occasional 'sport' by means of a snare.

I parked my car beside his house and looked over the fence. The front lawn of what was once a largish Victorian rectory was littered with the evidence of his calling – cement-mixers, dumper-trucks, a JCB and a couple of vans lay around in various stages of incompleteness. The Newt, in grass-stained overalls of impressive vintage, resembled an engineering version of a lion-tamer, as he lay across the wing of a battered Ford van, seemingly half-swallowed by the upraised bonnet.

''Lo, Rob,' he said, straightening up from the mechanical jaws, 'what you after, then?'
Close to, the Newt bears a passing, if somewhat bucolic, resemblance to the idol of his youth, Elvis Presley. He still retains the hairstyle of those days with slicked-back quiff and long sideburns. His hair is still naturally dark, and I have heard it said, though not to his face, that there is a touch of the Romany in the family.

'Just thought I'd drop in and have a chat,' I replied, with an effort at casualness.
The Newt wasn't fooled for a minute.
'Bugger off,' he said pleasantly, 'youm've had a whisper 'bout something or other. You bailiffs don't go a-visitin' social-like, leastways not to the likes o' me. What's up?'

There was really not much point in beating about the bush, so I told him about the net – without, of course, mentioning the informant. He stared at me for a moment and then, to my surprise, roared with laughter. Without another word, he took me by the arm with a large and oily paw and led me round to the back of the house. The back garden was in complete contrast to the front; whereas the front was more like a scrap-yard of mechanical litter, the back was immaculate – a vegetable and fruit garden that evinced much loving care and labour. The fine dark tilth of richly manured seed-beds contained sprouting occupants that had been planted with mathe-

Dipper

matical precision, and, alongside, early potatoes stood in neatly earthed-up lines. Hazel poles stood deftly tied to receive the clinging attentions of runner-beans and sweet-peas, while neat borders of alpines and heathers marked out the boundary between productive garden and slab path. Still chuckling, he indicated an area of freshly hoed soil covered with lines of yellow straw through which poked the contrasting dark green of strawberry runners. The whole bed was covered with an ancient fishing net, faded by immersion in sea and exposure to sunlight, pegged and tied at intervals to keep it some two feet above the ground.

'Thought I'd turned netsman, eh? That's the only net around here and you can take my word for it her wouldn't barely hold a minnow.'

I believed him. The net had been repaired so many times that there was little of the original left. A sudden gust would have split it in two.

'You won't catch me usin' a net, 'cos I never have an' never will. 'Tes no sport, see.'

On the way back, we stopped at the vehicle he'd been working on when I arrived.

'Don't want to buy 'er, do 'ee?' he asked. 'Be a nice little runner in a day or two. Two hundred for cash.'

I shook my head. Through the crudely brushed fading paintwork I could just distinguish the letters COUNTY COUNCIL. Seeing my glance Newt added, 'Goin' in for disposals, see. 'Andsome lot of money to be made at that game. Won't have no time fer the salmon for a

Roebuck with antlers
in velvet

while,' he added with a wink, then asked in the same breath, 'an' I s'pose it was that miserable old bastard nex' door who gabbed about th' net?'

I said nothing but he must have seen something in my face for he nodded in a satisfied manner.

'Thought so. Well, I'll settle up with the old sod one of these days. Never did get on with 'im since he pinched me brother's marbles at Whitchurch Primary School – an' that was a few year back . . . .'

It seemed an insignificant matter with which to begin a lifetime feud; however, time was getting on, so I left him to his thoughts of vengeance and headed once more for the river.

V

The Tavy and the Walkham meet at the aptly named Double Waters in a heavily wooded valley a couple of miles to the west of the old mining village of Horrabridge. Apart from the ever-present rush of water, it is a quiet and pleasant spot leading to some dramatic scenery where the Tavy, having been joined by its sibling, curves round into a wide and deep pool cutting through a steep and rocky gorge before running over a natural weir. At the spot where the two rivers join there is a handsome new rustic bridge and it is an ideal place to compare the character of the waters. The ancients called the Tavy the Dark One, no doubt referring to its depth and the fact that for much of its length it travels through steeply banked woodland which reflects off the surface of the water as a rippling blackness. At Double Waters this effect is most noticeable in the evening, when the long shadows have been cast and the river swirls powerfully towards the gorge. The Walkham also lives up to its old name, the Wandering One, and joins its elder brother with a splash and a rush, having meandered first to the south and then to the west before merging forces.

I had walked down to the little bridge along the Walkham having left my car on West Down, looking into likely pools for the absent fish, and now took the opportunity of walking upstream beside the Tavy. Here the bank is comparatively wide before sloping sharply up into the woods, and small cliffs jut out of the surrounding scrub. Not long ago it was rumoured that one of the local bad lads had harboured out in a small cave among these rocks while on unofficial leave-of-absence from an open prison. Out of curiosity I climbed up to have a look. Though I found no cave, there was a deep cleft in the rock with a man-made sill or parapet of large stones; it seemed as if the rumour might be true. A good spot, I thought, for an observation post on an APP – the Authority's acronym for an anti-poaching patrol.

I sat in the cosy eyrie and looked down on the river. With the sun having disappeared behind the wooded slopes and the water level so low, it was possible to look down into the pools below and see the torpedo-like silhouettes of fish holding station against the current. As far as I could make out they were all peal or sea trout – the ocean-going version of our brownie. Not a salmon to be seen.

There was a movement among the close woodland and scrub of the far bank. As I watched, a roe-buck emerged from the gathering shadows and stood motionless beside the flowing waters, every sense alert for danger. Detecting neither threatening movement nor sound or smell, the animal moved gracefully but cautiously along the bank. Just what he intended I never found out, for at that moment a blackbird shrilled alarm and the deer vanished with a leap into the refuge of the trees. Walking along my side of the river came the cause of the alarm, an angler laden with rod, bag and net. I recognized him as an enthusiastic if somewhat unsuccessful fisherman whose only fault was that he suffered from that well-known angling malady, 'tackle-itis'. This is a disease common in any sport which employs a modicum of equipment, particularly affecting the more modest performers. Instead of concentrating on the practice and study of the basic techniques and skills, their initial lack of success can, they believe, be blamed entirely on inadequate equipment. This ailment naturally makes the tackle-manufacturers very happy indeed; after all, more people in Britain fish than take part in any other sport.

I scrambled down the scree to meet him. If he was at all surprised to see a river warden appearing from out of the rocks some twenty feet above his head, he did not show it. He greeted me amiably, and proceeded to explain that his intention was to settle down and wait until dark and then 'have a crack at the peal'. I wished him luck and indicated the well-populated lies I had spotted from up in the rocks. I was then asked to admire his latest acquisitions, a ten-foot boron/carbon rod and an exotic self-retrieving fly-reel. I made the appropriate admiring noises and wondered if his bank-manager was a fisherman too. A vast box of flies, almost the size of a Victorian cutlery canteen, was produced from his capacious bag and my opinion sought. A four-drawered riot of colour was revealed; the box must have contained one example of virtually every salmon

'Voyagers of the Rain', as Ewan Clarkson called the ghostly forms of sea-trout as
they lie waiting for rain

and sea trout fly ever tied – and a few more besides! I picked out an Alexandra but this practical if mundane choice seemed to disappoint him.

'I read an article last week,' he began, and went on at considerable length about an exotic confection called a Ghillies' Glory; a creation of tinsel and feather of virulent hues that was guaranteed by the writer of the article to drive fish into a frenzy. Privately, I agreed; if the peal had any artistic taste and appreciation of form and colour they would not only be driven into a frenzy, but would probably stage a full-blooded riot.

'You see,' he continued, with the light of true conviction shining in his eyes,' the theory is . . . '

That's the charm of fishing – every angler has his own theory as to why the fish are or aren't biting, as to why one stretch should show more sport than another, and so on. My theory, for what it is worth, is that you cannot call yourself a true fisherman unless you do theorize; my contention being that if you are not actually fishing then you should at least be thinking about it. In the case of the so-called Ghillies' Glory (and here's another theory: somewhere there is an embittered old fishing writer whose sole job in life it is to dream up more and more ridiculous names for each and every fly and lure – how else to explain the Mondays' Child or the Dog Nobbler?) the idea was that the revolting colours and gaudy banding would fade in the dark to an altogether more natural lure in the absence of ultra-violet light – at least I think that was the gist of his long and rambling explanation. Like all the best fishing theories it sounded plausible, so I wished him luck and turned to go.

'By the way, the wife enjoyed your talk last Wednesday,' he added, 'I s'pose the sex-life of the salmon must have made a change from jam and Jerusalem.'

I stared at him blankly.

'The Women's Institute. You gave them a lecture on the life-cycle of the salmon.'

'Sorry – couldn't think what you were talking about for a moment. I don't like giving talks but they gave me a jolly good tea to make up for it.'

He sighed, and the enthusiasm that had previously shone on his features was replaced by a look of deep and bitter gloom.

'I know,' he said heavily. 'There wasn't a Digestive left when I got home for tea that evening.'

I wished him well and left him on the bank assembling his tackle.

The mellow light of the setting sun cast long shadows across the valley, fingers of approaching darkness touching the bracken-covered hillside. Woodsmoke hung in the still air, and further down the valley I heard the high clear sound of children's voices. It was time to go home – via the trap.

VI

I walked back, with the occasional pause to admire the displays of shrub and flower and well-regimented rows of vegetables.

One of the pleasures of walking the lower reaches of the rivers is the ability to be what I can only describe as a 'horticultural Peeping Tom'. As a bailiff, and with the permission of the various owners who may have a stretch of bank from as little as ten feet to as much as several miles in length, one is afforded the opportunity and privilege of surreptitiously enjoying other people's gardens. Proximity to running water seems to spur the creative gardener to even greater efforts and I am often amazed at the results. Often one will view a house from the road and it will appear as little more than a roof showing over the top of a hedge, bland and private. But see the back and garden of the same house from the opposite river bank, and the private side of the house reveals itself in an imaginative profusion of blooms and shrubs that tumble down to the water's edge. Whether stately gardens with impressive rolling lawns or cottage gardens with vegetables and flowers all happily mixed together, the variations seem endless.

I was never much of a gardener until I got married, when my wife viewed the rank weed-infested wasteland with some disfavour.

'What's that?' she inquired, gazing out of the back door with narrowed eyes.

'Er, it's a natural garden – a sort of nature reserve for butterflies and wild flowers and . . . '

'It's nothing of the sort,' she retorted, with some asperity. 'It's – it's just a tip.'

I said nothing but looked unhappily at the tangles of briar, the banks of nettles, the mounds of builders' rubble and the rusted remains of a wheelbarrow. She had a point.

Now, some years later, we have a cottage-garden that has become my pride and joy – and is still something of a nature reserve. Under the edge of the wood are the wild flowers: primrose, wood sorrel, snowdrops, bluebells, cyclamen, speedwell, viper's bugloss, bird's foot trefoil and ragged robin. Honeysuckle has entwined itself around the buddleia by the fence and, to balance this pretty

picture, I still retain a patch of nettles, some ragwort and a few brambles.

The net result – allied with conventional beds, a rockery, a lawn and a vegetable garden – is, to me, total enchantment. Like many of my fellow-men I have been converted; what was once a chore is now a delight, and I still have the butterflies.

I used their presence as an excuse not to garden, but butterflies, it would seem, respond to luxury; where they once existed in their hundreds, they are now in their thousands, and as the numbers have increased so have the species. Along with the red admirals, peacocks and tortoiseshells have come the small skippers, the brimstones, brown hairstreaks and the silver-washed fritillaries (I once counted 230 of these on the buddleia alone!), the meadow browns, the gatekeepers, small heaths and common blues.

I can think of no greater pleasure than to sit in the garden of a summer afternoon and watch the butterflies. Unless, of course, I had a trout rod in the other hand . . .

VII

The sodden little body lay outstretched on the bank. For the second time that day the trap had been sprung. Male and female had both succumbed – but in the case of the latter, not without protest,

Opposite: studies from the garden – grasses, speedwell, dandelion and campion

Campion

Sowing Plantain

I cannot remember being so moved as I was
last week at the Thyme when I saw a small
study by C Alexander. it contained in just
a few lines and washes the purity and genius
of a master of countryside and reading his
subject.
    I'm not suggesting that these studies are
comparable but my concept is now pointing
in the right direction.
    Grasses, speedwell, dandelion, campion, all
from the garden. 14.6.83
                    Robin Armstrong

Cuckoo Spit

for several of her needle-like teeth showing in a rictus of death were broken, and scored metal bore shiny witness to the power of those fangs.

I was about to toss the silvery-grey corpse aside when a thought occurred to me. There was something about the colour that reminded me of . . . but my memory refused to co-operate until triggered by a sound from downstream – the splash of a fish head-and-tailing. Of course, the Olive Dun! The recipe called for 'dyed medium olive seal's fur'. Surely mink would do as well?

For the purposes of rounding off this account, I would like to have reported that it made an excellent substitute and caught a fish on its first cast. Unfortunately, this was not so. The fur took the colour well, but from then on proved an abject failure, lacking the stiffness of seal-fur. It was lost on its first outing, caught in the gnarled branches of an old oak as a result of a misdirected back-cast – and, no, I didn't climb up and get it down.

CHAPTER FIVE

'HE'M A NICE LIDDLE RIVER'

I

T HE steel blade bit deeply into the peaty bank and, with a levering motion of the long hickory handle, the turf fell free. George, my boss, carried it over to the dam and fitted it into place, grassy side uppermost, using the back of the shield-shaped spade to tamp it down. Finished, he regarded his implement critically.

'Can't beat 'un,' he remarked. ''Twas the old Cornish shovel that built Americky,' he added, with a sideways glance at Dave. Getting no immediate response, he went back to slicing out further turves.

When I was a kid, one of my favourite expeditions was to the glades and copses of Pett's Wood, courtesy of London Transport and the number 229 bus. A bunch of us would run yelling and screaming through the trees, upsetting the locals in the midst of their comfortable middle-class perambulations and exciting their small dogs into a shrill frenzy of protective yapping. This appalling behaviour ('damn'd young hooligans') would then be followed by a

long and usually inconclusive game of Cops and Robbers, English and Germans, or Cowboys and Indians. Battles successfully concluded, we would then embark on my favourite pastime – building dams across one of the little streams. Constructive vandalism, I suppose you could call it. Branches of young saplings would be snapped off and laid across the stream and reinforced with gravel, clods of earth torn away from the bank and, best of all, handfuls of wet sloppy mud excavated from the shallows on the principle of one for the dam and one to throw at your best friend. A successful dam was one that caused the riverlet to flood its banks and spill on to the paths, forcing people to detour from their walks into the undergrowth.

We cared little for the natural life of the area, other than trying to catch the little darting sticklebacks in jam-jars or having an adolescent snigger at the piggyback antics of frogs and toads in season; the dam was all – even if some gum-booted resident was going to kick it down the moment we had left. The wetter and muddier we got, the more fun it all seemed to be.

Today's dam is a rather different affair, for the benefit of the natural life of the area, with particular reference to the salmon and freshwater fish with whose welfare we, as river wardens, are entrusted. The small, fast-flowing river has been trying to cut corners where we are working and persistent erosion has resulted in the formation of an ox-bow lake. Eventually the remorseless rush will push through to form a cutting and create a tiny island doomed to be swept away in the course of one or more spates, while the outside bend of the river is filled in by deposited silt. In two or three years, a mere hiccup in the life of the aeons-old stream, there will be little trace of the bend which once slowed the merciless course of water and, in so doing, set up an oxygen-rich turbulence flowing over the gravel beds downstream from the deflection. An ideal spawning ground for salmon and sea trout.

Our small dam will be little more permanent than those early constructions in the London woods of thirty years ago, but if it succeeds for only a few months then it will have served its purpose, for by then the fish will have bred and the waters can be allowed to wash it away.

George thumped the last of the peaty turves into place with a flourish of the long-handled spade and eyed his handiwork critically.

Silver Washed Fritillary from sightings in the garden during 1983

Bramble

pupa

Silver washed Fritillary, from eggings
in the garden during 1983, the
Purple Emperor was one which I
reared from pupa supplied by
John McFeely, all which emerged
were female. The pupa jumped
alarmingly when touched on the
tip.   Robin Armstrong 1984

Purple Emperor ♀

'Proper job,' he said, patting the grassy-topped bank with satisfaction. 'Just have to run the old Flymo across the top, and her'll be finished', and, roaring with laughter, he lumbered over to join Dave for a smoke. I grinned at his retreating back, amused by the thought of a rotary lawn-mower buzzing merrily among the boulders of this harsh and ancient landscape.

II

The river Walkham, the 'Wandering One', starts its meandering high on Dartmoor between the granite outcrops of Devil's Tor to the east and Lynch Tor to the west. Tumbling over boulder and slab through the windswept tussocky moorland it veers westward under the shadow of Cocks Hill then dips to the south between Roos Tor and Great Mis Tor before vanishing into the oak-hung Walkham valley to the south of Merrivale. After a fast, rocky run between the trees, the river begins to live up to its old name and meanders cheerfully to the south-west where it joins its bigger sister, the Tavy, and together they join the Tamar and flow via Plymouth Sound to the sea.

Hen harriers

Standing stone at Merrivale

Dartmoor is the mother to most of the principal rivers of Devon with the exception of the Tamar, Exe and Torridge, but of all the rivers that have their source in the barren uplands, the Walkham is my favourite. I live beside it and am servant to it. I never tire of its changing scenery, its riffles and rapids, weirs and waterfalls, its quiet tree-hung pools and shallow gravel-bottomed stretches – but of all its tumbling, twisting length, the area I find the most attractive and fascinating is the upper Walkham valley from Ward bridge, close to my home, to the moorland stretch where we were now working.

On a sunlit spring day like today, it seems an eminently peaceful spot. The river chuckles past, fresh from its source in the bog and bracken, runs through ling, heath and gorse, followed by close-cropped moorland pasture, before disappearing into the tree-lined fringes of the upper valley. The ring of pick and shovel as Dave and George struggle to extricate a particularly obstinate small boulder has been heard in these parts before. Once, before people first came to the moor, the woodland reached up to the slopes of the tors. The requirements of early man for fuel, building and agriculture soon denuded the slopes and left only pockets of woodland. Incidentally, the title of 'Dartmoor Forest' merely signifies a royal hunting ground, a title bestowed upon the central area of the moor since the days of the Black Prince.

Merrivale is now a sleepy hamlet, the only signs of industry being the quarry and farming, with the pub catering to the tourist trade in summer. Just when – and who – the first settlers were in the area is a matter for academic argument, but it is certain that man was well ensconced by the Bronze Age (approximately 2000 to 500 B.C.) for traces of dwellings, graves and possibly their religion are to be found in the area in the shape of stone rows, circles and cairns. It was the discovery that copper, alloyed with some 10 per cent of tin, produced bronze to make weapons, that probably established the fortunes of the early settlers on Dartmoor. I say probably, because the first documentary evidence of tin-mining does not occur until 1156, many centuries after the founding of the first known settlements. But it would be strange if those early settlers did not take advantage of the veins and lodes that must have been exposed by the action of weathering on the rock. Certainly the medieval tinners did, and Merrivale and the upper Walkham valley must have experienced something of a 'Tin Rush', for their workings, largely grown over and forgotten, litter the landscape to this day. The river not only gave up ore from its bed – washed by the weathering process – but lent its power to the water-wheels used to crush the rock to extract the ore and to power the bellows used in the smelting process. Close to our makeshift dam lie the remains of an ancient 'blowing-house' or smelting works; the troughed floor into which the molten metal ran is clearly visible.

It must have been eerie to see the smoke of a thousand little furnaces rising from the combes and hillsides; the scene at night would have done nothing to assuage the old beliefs that the moor was the Devil's own country, with the fires winking redly and occasionally shooting out sparks and flames as air rushed through the charcoal-fired furnaces.

Boom-time beside the river – but such days are long gone and the water flows on down the upper reaches, no longer tainted by the mole-like activities of the miners.

'Hats off,' said George.

I looked around, bewildered, until I saw what he was pointing at. Down the river, at a stately but steady pace, came the swollen corpse of a sheep.

'Been dead awhile,' said Dave. There was little doubt he was right.

'Brings tears to your eyes, that does,' and George wrinkled his nose in disgust as the gaseous remains grounded gently on the pebbles of our newly preserved spawning ground. The corpse was checked only momentarily before it spun off with the current and vanished round the bend, one stiffened leg waving a jaunty farewell.

'Your turn, Robbie.'

Sometimes there is a distinct disadvantage to being the most junior bailiff – especially where dead sheep are concerned. I wandered off in reluctant pursuit to pull the remains ashore. Corpses are an unfortunate fact of river life – much appreciated by the growing fish

Fly agaric, not very common in the Walkham Valley. I found these in some birch
plantations at Togoland on the Tavy

but regarded with considerably less enthusiasm by myself. It was while I was pulling the noisome sodden weight ashore, holding my breath and staring fixedly upwards, that I saw the falcon; not just any old falcon, but *the* falcon, a peregrine. It was a male, a tiercel, and sat calmly on a rock among the quarry spoil that heaped the opposite bank. He regarded me for a moment with unblinking eye, then returned his attention to the limp body that lay clutched below one curling talon. A pale grey feather drifted down on the slight breeze as the curved beak tore at the breast of a wood-pigeon. Peregrines are not common to the moor, preferring the cliffs and combes of the north coast of Devon and Cornwall, and I had never seen one at such close quarters before. We were less than ten feet apart, separated only by a narrow-gutted section of the river. He seemed remarkably unconcerned by my presence and I wondered if he was a half-trained bird escaped from some falconer, or perhaps he merely took me for some larger hawk settling down to dine off an equally large and woolly prey.

A spade rang on rock. The bird hunched and swivelled, every sense alert. The sound came again, and with a 'kek-kek-kek' of annoyance the peregrine took off and flicked rapidly down the valley. Strange that he hadn't seemed upset by my proximity, though metal against stone had frightened him off. I went back to tell the others.

'Well, you'm got a big enough nose, anyways,' observed Dave when I recounted my theory of being mistaken for another hawk. George laughed, unkindly I thought, and said, 'Seen a few o' they over the years. Where be to?'

I pointed down the valley.

'Likely gone to one o' they old quarries. Have a look on your way back; maybe a pair around. Now give a hand here and we'll get this side finished, then have a bite.'

III

A shadow flicked over the landscape and, before the senses could properly take in the racing shade, was accompanied by a blast of sound as a low-flying jet flashed over the crest of the hill, swung in a great arc to the south of the granite bulk of King's Tor, diminishing into a black speck hanging in a blue kerosene haze before finally vanishing, a low rumbling roar receding into the background rush of running water.

As the first roar faded, a second aircraft flashed over in noisy pursuit.

'He'll never catch 'un,' remarked George, straightening up and grinding a meaty fist into the small of his back. The sheep and ponies simply ignored this twentieth-century intrusion and went on nibbling at the over-cropped grass. The distant rumble of the planes faded, to be replaced by the faint and intermittent sounds of small-arms fire to the north of us. The 'pop-pop' sounds died away after a few moments.

'Short battle, that.'

'Bit one-sided if you ask me. Bloody great aircraft against a few rifles . . . Tisn't hardly fair.'

'Well, you know the old saying, Dave – if'n you can't take a joke you shouldn't have joined.'

The two strategists leant on the shovels and gazed towards the military exercise area, hidden from our view by the massive bulk of Great Mis Tor. I kept quiet, my only military experience being confined to the Scouts.

Ignoring the sounds of mock-battle, I scouted around for some more substantial stones to buttress the dam. The remains of a collapsed wall, now reduced to little more than a series of humps in the coarse grass, offered itself as a source of new material.

As I levered the roughly dressed stones away from the clinging

undergrowth, it occurred to me that we take the rectangular fili-
gree pattern of walling that lies over the hillsides like some great
spider's web totally for granted – yet its presence, squaring off the
slopes and uplands, bears witness to the continuous effort and
struggle of those in the past to enclose, clear and improve the harsh
soil. Miles of these walls, extending well into the heart of the moor,
now lie crumbling and abandoned, offering an undisturbed habitat
for all manner of flora and fauna.

There is a section of wall, not far from our cottage, which runs
from the top of the hill at Sampford Spiney down to the river – a
distance of some three-quarters of a mile. It is just one wall among
thousands, yet one cannot but marvel at the industry that went into
its creation. The base stones are massive slabs of roughly dressed
granite, the largest of which are some four feet long, two feet wide
and two feet thick. Whether these large stones were quarried on
the spot or brought from elsewhere, I do not pretend to know – but
I remain impressed at the result. The wall is of fairly standard construction and differs from its neighbours only in the size of the
stones employed; even the top row is made up of neatly dressed six-
to eight-inch cubes. It is not an old wall – probably late Victorian
since it marks the boundary of an estate of comparatively recent
creation – yet it remains my favourite, since in walking its length, a
cross-section of the valley's treasures is revealed.

From the top, the view is east: the rocky outcrop of King's Tor
seemingly surmounted by the BBC aerial at North Hessary Tor
which actually lies over a mile further on; the abandoned quarry
workings at Foggintor, just to the south, which resemble nothing so
much as giant terracing; and, finally, the mound of Ingra Tor lying
to the south-east. Below this humped skyline is a network of small
fields – an agricultural chessboard – which merge into the woodland
of the lower slopes. In spring, which is my favourite time to walk
the wall, the boundaries of the higher fields show signs of
encroachment by the pervasive bracken – a brown mantle of last
year's growth covers the high ground and spills down into the
neatly delineated squares of grazing. Once, the bracken was kept at
bay for it was cut and dried for winter bedding, but this is rarely
the custom today. Unfortunately, the plant grows only in the better
moorland soils and is a constant nuisance to the grazier since it is
both poisonous to animals in quantity and a harbourer of ticks
(walk through bracken in the summer and you lay yourself open to

I probably see more badgers than any other large mammal – it must be the hours
I keep

106

Badger, I probably see more
badgers than any other large
mammal, must be the hours
I keep.   Robin Armstrong

attack by the parasitical little blood-suckers; the female of the species engorged with blood resembles nothing so much as an obscene grape). There is an old saying that runs 'plough heather find copper; plough furze, find silver; plough fern and find gold' – indicating the plant's preference for good soil. Both the furze and the heather are of more value to animals since they contain vital trace-elements, brought up from the sub-soil by the root system.

The field system is identical on our side of the valley, and as one follows the wall down the hill towards the river the shoots of young bracken can be seen uncurling from the earth like miniature bishop's croziers. But in spring, the emergence of this pest is over-shadowed by the true glory of the woodlands that march on the other side of the wall – the bluebells, a carpet of smoky blue that erupts through the thick leaf-mould to delight the eye.

Further down the hill, the hygienically-minded badgers from one of the many local setts have established their outdoor lavatory – a series of shallow scrapes that lie alongside the wall, each containing neatly-deposited dung. The wall itself sags somewhat dramatically at this point into a deep indentation in the cropped grass – evid-ence of the subterranean activities of Brock since the sett runs under the wall with large piles of bedding and freshly excavated earth heaped on either side.

This particular area seems equally attractive to the ubiquitous black slug whose dried trails criss-cross the moss and lichen-covered stones. Found throughout the valley, their particular concentration in this area has always puzzled me and I have yet to find the answer. Doubtless the badgers appreciate their presence, though.

The subsidence has caused the spaces between the neatly-laid stones to open up, and at the lower end a wren has established a nest deep in the heart of the granite blocks. When I first saw the little bird flitting in and out of the fissure, ferrying building materi-als with all the fervour of the true DIY enthusiast, I gave little for his chances. Surely a weasel or rat would polish him and his family off with one well-timed visit? But, thankfully, it would seem that I was wrong for this is the third season that the bird has been nesting in the wall – I can only assume that the entrance to the nest is both minute and surrounded by rock.

On the other side of the wall is a beech-wood; a surprising find on the acid high ground, yet the trees have survived the gales and the cold since they were first planted and are now well formed and mature, standing guard over the glade. Primroses grow in profusion out of and along this side of the wall and a wood-pigeon clappers into the air, disturbed from scratching in the dense carpet of slowly decomposing leaves and shells. Little grows under the tall trees except a scattering of bird's nest orchids and fungus – boletus and common ganoderma. Later in the year the poisonous fly agaric is to be found in the narrow strip of birch plantation that forms a boundary between the lower slopes of the beeches and the ancient stunted oaks that continue down to the river.

The slope of the wall steepens at this point, with marshy land on one side and a drier but rock-littered woodland on the other.

Halfway down the incline is the only collapsed section of the wall, due not to the mining activities of badgers but to those of rabbits. The whole area is pockmarked with their holes and the earth below must resemble nothing so much as a giant Swiss cheese. On the woodland side of the warren a fox has moved in, enlarging the rabbits' original efforts to form an earth; doubtless on the principle of the lazy shopper living next to the supermarket.

The rabbits' initial demolition job has been exacerbated by the mountaineering activities of the Blackfaced sheep, who appear to regard every wall and fence as a challenge to their independent natures. They will butt, scrape and struggle their way over, or through, any obstacle in their path. I have even seen one group using the dead body of a ram which had caught his curling horns in wire and broken his neck, as a stepping-stone to surmount the fence. Neither are they dependent on brute force and ignorance, for they have long since mastered the art of crossing cattle-grids by rolling over them.

Whereas the wall of the top and middle sections is on comparatively well-drained ground and accessible to sunlight, the same cannot be said of the lower section which squats athwart a bed of ooze,

Brown hare

held up by the massive outcrops of granite which reveal themselves as bare grey patches in the poor grass. The inhabitants differ accordingly – common lizards, harvest mice and slow-worms in the drier apartments and toads, frogs and bank voles in the damp basement. Moonwort and pennywort grow in the crevices throughout the wall, as do towering foxgloves, but the real attraction lies at the bottom of the hill among the ancient oaks, where great green mounds of cushion moss *(Leucobryum glaucum)* are heaped against the wall and extend for a considerable distance among the trees, spongy, virulently green heaps of moist moss. Indicative of the age of the dwarf oaks are the pendants of lungwort on the tree-bark which bear a parasitical resemblance to the oak's own leaves.

The wall ends some four feet from the undercut bank in a clump of rhododendron bushes, their roots tangled and twisted through the gaps in the base-stones.

It is just one wall, one length, of the thousands of miles of walling that run over the English countryside; an artificial division, perhaps, of the landscape, but a home, a refuge and a larder to the animals, plants and insects that inhabit its length.

IV

As the sounds of guns and planes faded away, George announced that it was time for a bite to eat. It was perfect weather to sit beside the river with a sandwich or pasty, admire our handiwork and enjoy the spring sunshine. The sky was a pale talcum blue with not a cloud to be seen, and the plash and chuckle of the water was interrupted only by the rustle of grease-proof paper and the irate ticking of a cock-wren warning us away from his tangled territory somewhere in the heart of a nearby bramble thicket.

A remarkable little bird is the humble Titty Todger, with an energy, aggression and song out of all proportion to his minute frame. The nest or nests – for the wren is an avid civil engineer – is a domed, woven structure, and on the moor is often found in such thickets or among crevices, like the one in the weathered granite of the wall. Like the robin, wrens seem to have a friendly indifference towards the presence of people, and by the time I had unwrapped my first cheese-and-chutney sandwich, his excited threats had changed to liquid song.

Those who ascribe anthropomorphic traits to our song-birds would do well to remember that the human vices of sulkiness and

Primroses: a sure sign of spring

idleness do not appear to be part of the creature's character. A bird's song is its emotional barometer and can run the gamut through warning, aggression and fear, to the happier expressions of love and joy, with hardly a pause for reflection – and all this is coupled with the never-ending routines of feeding, nesting and mating. The wren's busy and courageous behaviour contrasted sharply with another, far larger bird which had also been disturbed by our presence on the river. The clink and thunk of pick and shovel had put up a lumbering grey heron who had been standing by the shallows some fifty to a hundred yards upstream; with neck tucked back and slow beating wings he had flown to a point half-way up the hillside and was now almost indistinguishable from the surrounding lumps of granite. From this vantage-point he glared down at us, occasionally taking short hopping flights to one side or another, but not daring to return to the shallows where the little trout and samlets (young salmon) darted; the wren, meanwhile, stayed put and his clear gushing song was a happy accompaniment to the sounds of the river.

'Spindle-shanked old bugger,' says George, noting my interest in the heron. 'Powerful good poacher, though. Wonder he don't fly over the hill down to the trout farm, 'stead of scratchin' around here.'

'Got nets up,' says Dave, whose comments tend to be short and to the point. He makes a natural foil to the ebullient Cornishman, and the two resemble a classic comedy duo from the era of music hall. The slow, solid and somewhat taciturn Devonian paired with the equally large but extrovert man from 't'other side of the Tamar' whose marvellous rambling stories are topped by Dave's dry one-liners. They have worked beside the river for years and known it throughout their lives. Occurrences and happenings which are fascinating to me are taken for granted by these two who have acted as my mentors; yet they are not the least blasé about their depth of knowledge and are as happy to pass on their lore as to acknowledge any new facts that may have escaped them.

Mention of the heron's predilection for thieving gluttony prompts George to recount a story.

'Seein' that heron just standin' there like an old stone gatepost reminds me of ol' Long John from up Bridestowe way – you 'member him, Dave?'

'He came from Hatherleigh,' is Dave's only comment.

Unabashed, George continues: 'Master poacher, wer old Long John. Took fish all his life an' never got caught. Still poachin' at the age of eighty-four . . .'

'Eighty-five, and then only 'cos he were blind.'

'Eighty-four, eighty-five, what's the difference? Anyway, you mind Janner, Robbie? The feller from the estate who's only ten bob in the pound?'

I nodded. No matter how many times I've sat with these two yarning, they always contrive to tell me something new. Janner is a poacher I've caught several times, and although I wouldn't rate his mental capabilities as low as George does, it is true that he is remarkably unimaginative when it comes to excuses. I once collared him walking beside the Tavy at two in the morning carrying an eight-pound fresh-run salmon with the snare-noose still round its tail. When I asked him where he had got it, he wrinkled his fore-

Heron studies from birds seen at Hartley trap in November

head and after a few minutes' deep cogitation volunteered the information: 'Some bloke give it me.' Since he was covered in fish-scales, had a torch and another snare in his capacious pockets, I found it somewhat difficult to give him the benefit of the doubt. West Devon has more than its share of eccentrics, but fish-giving philanthropists are not among them.

George continued. Janner, it appeared, was fed up with getting nicked. He had the basic skills to poach the fish, but somehow or other – it seemed to him – he just had the bad luck always to get caught. Hearing tales of the great Long John ('eighty-five and never been caught'), he thought he would visit the old boy and see if he could discover his secret. Over several pints the blind poacher reminisced, and in the course of so doing gave young Janner various hints. As far as the befuddled Janner could understand (for his capacity for beer was below that of the octogenarian) these were three in number and were, first, always poach at night, second, always poach alone and, third, at the slightest unusual sound run in the opposite direction from the river bank, throw oneself flat and do not, on any account, move.

'Providin' you don't move, boy,' said the ancient, 'you'll be safe. Many's the time the bailiffs have near trod on me – but Oi didn't move and they din't see Oi. Thank'ee, boy, Oi'll have another o' the same.'

A weaving Janner made his way back home, determined that the following night should see the first of a great many successes, perhaps even the start of a legend ('Remember old Janner? Never been caught in all these years . . . How old? Well he got his telegram from the Queen at least two years ago'). Twenty-four hours later saw him beside the Walkham with torch and snare.

His luck was in, and after half an hour's work he had landed two handsome peal. He had just missed a fine cock salmon, but he knew where he could almost certainly find another in a tangle of tree-roots where the bank was severely undercut. Reaching the spot he lay down, head and shoulders hanging over the bank, looking for his quarry, when, to his horror, he heard twigs snap, and thorns scrape on rain-proof clothing. The bailiffs! Rule three came to his aid, and he dropped the fish and took to his heels away from the river. He heard a shout behind him and a crashing in the under-growth. He reached a small clearing, threw himself flat and struggled to control his frantic breathing as he lay on the dew-sodden grass. Pressing himself against the earth he concentrated with all his will to remain motionless.

'He lay still, all right,' said George, 'just as still as that old heron.

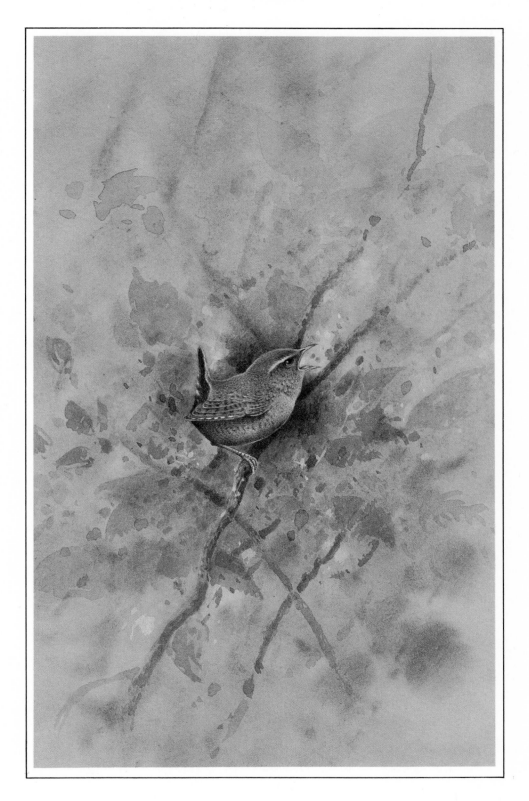

Wren

Unless you knew he were there you'd never ha' seen him.'

'So you didn't catch him?' I asked.

'We did that,' grunted Dave.

'How?'

Dave and George exchanged glances.

'Told you he wasn't all there upstairs, boy. Janner ran for it all right, and he lay still all right, but the only thing he did wrong was to leave his torch on . . . '

V

By now, the little dam had become a remarkably substantial structure with the addition of a sodden old railway sleeper, discovered half-hidden in the sedge, laid snugly along the bank of turves and stones; further evidence of man's incursions into the bleak uplands. The apparently barren hillside yielded several further aids to construction in the shape of lengths of rusted angle-iron and corrugated sheeting. The finishing touches were provided by some smooth flat boulders taken from the river by George and Dave.

In the meantime, I set about raking the gravel spawning ground free of silt, and adding suitable pebbles uncovered during the turf-cutting operations. The peat-tainted water flowed strongly past me, moulding my waders to my legs as I stood in midstream doing my best to decorate the salmon's boudoir in what I hoped the fish might consider to be an attractive manner. The water was so cold that my hands began to ache after only a few moments' immersion and it became increasingly hard to see just what a pair of fish might find so desirable about a few hundred pebbles or so.

Just as I was beginning to envy the other two at their more strenuous task setting the boulders on top of the final layer of turves, there was a loud ringing crack and a yell. In attempting to lever free a useful-looking rock, George had broken the shaft of his spade and sat disconsolate, glaring at the length of broken hickory in his hand. A wintry smile flitted across Dave's face.

'So much for America, my 'andsome.' He gave a bark of laughter and manoeuvred his own stone into position.

The dam was finished. We gathered up our tools (and parts of tools) and made our way up the short, steep hillside. I turned and looked back. From above, the effect of our work could clearly be seen. The stream cut cleanly round the side of the dam to swirl and gush on its course down to the sea, no longer extracting silt from the now land-locked ox-bow lake and clouding the bright clear spawning beds. It wouldn't last long, of course; another big spate would cause the river to rise well above the level of today's work. The evidence lies in the fact that previous spates have left thin lines of dead reeds and other vegetation running in a tell-tale column through the water-combed grasses of the bank. Still, so long as it stayed for a week or so, it would have removed just one of the obstacles that face the salmon and sea trout in their Herculean task of procreation.

Standing beside me, Dave said something that, no matter how many times I have heard it before, never ceases to puzzle me – though on this occasion it made a strange sense. I make no claim to be an authority on dialect, but in the years I have lived in Devon I have noticed a remarkably random use of gender in referring to objects, though with a strong preference towards the use of the feminine or neuter. This leads to rather endearing expressions such as 'Her be a proper job' or ''Tis a proper job' when referring, for instance, to something inanimate, whether it is a tractor or a pint of beer. The exception, particularly to Dave and George, seemed to be that beside which we earn our living.

'He'm a nice liddle river,' said Dave.

Alevin, parr and fry

CHAPTER SIX

BY FAIR MEANS...

I

THERE are times when discretion is definitely the better part of valour, and yesterday was one of those times. It was market day in Tavistock and a cheerful, heaving crowd of people greeted each other as if they'd not met for months instead of just last week. Farmers and their livestock thronged the pens and auction sheds on the hill, while their wives shopped, drank coffee and gossiped in the town below; a centuries-old ritual of rural life. Henry I, in 1105, granted the first charter for a market to be held every Friday and the tradition still continues. Home produce of every kind is sold under the cover of the pannier market and beside the road skirting this building flows the river that gives the town its name – the Tavy. It is a generous river for its waters have long provided people in the area with food, drink and power. Salmon, trout and eel are taken from the river for the table, water flows along leats cut into the upper reaches to quench the thirst of man and beast at remote farmsteads, and turbines are spun for the generation of electricity, replacing the old water-wheels that were used to crush ores, grind corn and power the weaving looms.

I left my car not far from the cattle-market, walked down the hill enjoying the spring sunshine, over the abbey bridge, and turned towards the library. I glanced over the low granite wall at the river flowing smoothly some eight feet below. Although we had had rain the previous week the level had dropped significantly and the water had cleared to its familiar peaty-brown tint. Two small boys were sitting on the wall opposite the library, cheap glass-fibre spinning rods in hand casting their lures with great optimism if little skill. I doubted that they were in possession of either licence or permit but it seemed somewhat irrelevant in view of the fact that the river was so low. Any sizeable fish would have taken advan-

Fresh salmon in the roots

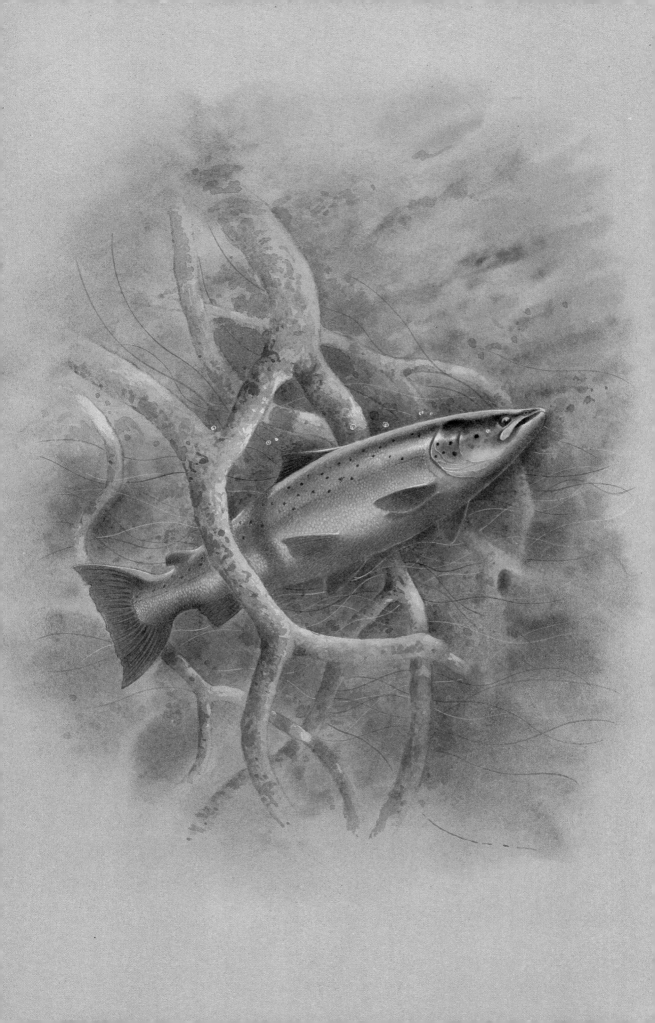

tage of last week's spate to move upriver; I intended to have a word with the youngsters once I had returned the armful of library books.

As I watched, one of the boys cast his lure, which appeared to be a small red Devon, straight across the Tavy to the opposing bank where it immediately snagged in the branches of a small willow. The elder of the two, who couldn't have been much more than twelve, immediately jumped in and waded across – the water hardly came up to his knees. Splashing around and yelling instructions to his companion to 'let they line goo slack, Gary – 'tis all in a tangle' seemed an unlikely way to attract the attentions of a healthy salmon in possession of its wits.

I went into the library but scarcely had I handed over the books when the swing doors burst open and two children rushed in in a state of high excitement.

'Mum, Mum, there's a boy outside an' he's caught an enormous fish. It's huge. Come and see . . . '

The library emptied rapidly, and I was left stranded in the rush to see the 'enormous fish'. By the time I got outside there were at least a dozen or so spectators craning over the wall. It was an extraordinary sight. The smaller of the two boys, having freed his lure from the drooping clutches of the willow, was now balanced on the wall like an apprentice tightrope walker – his uncertain equilibrium due to the fact that his little six-foot rod was almost bent double under the strain from downstream. I found a vantage-point and looked over; the taut line ran from the tip of the quivering rod to a spot close to the opposite bank which lay deep in shadow from the overhanging foliage. As I watched, a part of the shadow seemed to become detached, then with a liquid *thwack!* erupted from the water to metamorphose into a salmon, arching itself clear of its natural element in an effort to free itself from the nagging attentions of the lure and line. *Salmo salar* – the sea leaper, the Bar of Silver – fresh run from the estuary and twelve pounds if he was an ounce.

People were hurrying up every moment. They were streaming out of the pannier market, the ambulance station, the shops and cafés. Shouts of encouragement and advice rose on all sides.

'Give 'im line, boy, give 'im line.'

'Watch it! 'E'll goo downstream, f'sure.'

''Tis a proper fish an' no mistake. Wonder the lad can hold him.'

Their faces shone with enthusiasm. It would seem as if within the sturdy soul of every Tavonian there dwelt a fisherman.

The contest was evenly matched: the slight strength and inferior equipment of the boy was balanced by the fact that the fish was handicapped in the shallow water. Had it been deeper I had no doubt that the line would have been snapped long ago; in fact I was surprised that it had lasted as long as it had. The young Izaac Walton was still perched precariously on top of the wall, while his partner capered in the shallows within splashing distance of their quarry, adding his advice and encouragement to that of the crowd. Suddenly, the line went slack and the crowd gasped in disappointment. The four-foot fisherman, relieved of his counterbalance, was in imminent danger of toppling backwards off the wall when a helping adult hand from the throng steadied him. The salmon, thwarted of his natural inclination to run downstream, had surged forward in the opposite direction, heading for the deep lie where I had first seen him.

'Reel in, Gary,' shrieked his sopping accomplice.

'Reel in, reel in,' echoed the crowd.

The boy swayed, recovered himself, and did just that. Using the flex of the rod to pull at right angles to the fish's run, and winding like a maniacal organ-grinder, he managed to frustrate the salmon's intentions just on the edge of deeper water. A collective sigh of relief went up, but the danger was not over yet. Deprived of depth, the springer lived up to its name, scattering water and gravel in a series of arching leaps. Then once again it moved down with the current and the boy began to shuffle along the wall, keeping pace with the foaming commotion in midstream. In spite of myself, I was impressed. The lad had a deft touch despite his uncertain perch which he had to maintain since, had he climbed down on to the roadway, it was doubtful if he would have been able to see over the top of the wall, while in the other direction was a dangerous jump for one so small. He had the drag adjusted on his small fixed-spool reel to a nicety and then made the best of his small stiff rod by pulling in smoothly rather than in a series of harsh pumping motions. It seemed to me, though, that the odds were still in favour of the fish, which, unlike the boy, showed little signs of tiring.

Another point in the salmon's favour was a series of small rapids, or riffles, ten yards or so further downstream, followed by a pool. If it could gain ground, either the projecting rocks would sever the line or the deeper water would enable it to take full advantage of its amazing fighting powers by diving and running with the current. Just before the rapid, there was a smaller pool close to the far bank, just big enough to take the fish. As a fisherman, I would have tried to play the salmon in the direction of that, and as a bailiff I would then have removed the barbs and allowed the fish to go. I opened my mouth – and closed it again. I was not the only one to spot the dangers of the riffle.

'Get the fish across, lad – give the rod to yer mate . . .'

'Let 'im 'ave more line . . .'

'No, no, keep it toight . . .'

There seemed to be as many opinions as there were spectators, and they must have numbered well over the hundred. The boy was very tired now, and the rod trembled in his hands as he fought to keep an even sidestrain. His lower lip stuck out and it seemed that tears of frustration were not far away. Worse, it was evident that the reel was giving way under the strain; line was being ripped off the spool in uneven jerks and surges. He called out something to the boy in the stream who responded by splashing his way back up to the spot where they had left their modest tackle. He returned carrying a net, not the long-handled wide-mouthed variety normally used by salmon fishermen, but a cheap keep-net – a tubular device favoured by coarse fishermen and held apart by plastic rings. I could not see how this was going to help since its mouth was far too narrow to take a salmon some three feet long which was leaping around convulsively.

The little reel had now jammed and the rod bowed and whipped like a live thing. The salmon, feeling the restriction and perhaps sensing freedom as it neared the riffle, redoubled its efforts. A galvanic leap in an attempt to break free was thwarted only by his adversary quickly dropping the rod tip and taking a teetering run along the wall towards the fish. The lad in the water was now almost directly downstream of the glistening salmon, standing below the two largest jutting rocks which formed the main watercourse through to the deeper water. Suddenly the tip ring of the rod snapped clean off. Surely the line must break as well? The crowd evidently thought so, for there was a collective sigh of disappointment and sympathy. There was another flurry of spray and foam as the fish sought to take advantage of the sudden, if small, amount of slack. The boy lowered the rod again and then, to my surprise, tucked it under his arm while he opened a penknife that he had taken from the pocket of his shorts. He took hold of the rod again, applied sidestrain across the river, so that the salmon was poised above the gap between the worn rocks and then, when the line was humming taut, he took his knife and cut the line. There was a gasp, and the fish, feeling release for the first time in some twenty minutes, flicked around and swam smoothly and strongly through the gap – and straight into the waiting keep-net!

The audience went mad; cheers, applause and hoots of laughter

Walkham salmon parr, showing the very distinct coloration: an almost
purple sheen

greeted this piscatorial master-stroke. The fish's captor ignored the
hubbub and, taking a large pebble from the river bed, dealt his
frantically struggling victim the *coup de grâce*, then waded to the
bank heaving the net behind him.

The crowd, now numbering over two hundred, pressed around
the two boys and their trophy, tousling their hair and patting their
backs in a generous display of congratulation. Someone held the
fish up beside the boys as another took their photograph.

Eventually the crowd began to thin out and the field was left to
the fellow-enthusiasts.

'Catch him on a red minnow, eh?'

'Fresh-run, too. See the lice? Must have come up on the last
spate.'

'Cock-fish. Must be twelve pounds, mebbe more.'

Then came the inevitable question, casually posed by a burly fellow with his hands in his pockets.

'How much do you want for him, lads? Tell you what, I'll give you a fiver; what d'yer say?'

Their fellow-anglers angrily turned in the boys' defence.

'A fiver? Don't be bloody silly, man. Fresh salmon's worth more'n two quid a pound in the shops.'

The boys stood mute, watching the adults arguing above them. Cornered, the big man appealed to them.

'Well, come on, lads, 'ow much do yer want?'

They exchanged glances, then the elder one spoke.

'Don't want to sell,' he said softly. 'Want to take 'im back ter our Mum.'

This met with general approbation and the boys were left to themselves. I remained leaning against the wall as they gathered together their modest tackle and picked up the silvery fish, a limp and glazed-eyed remnant shedding scales on their clothes.

'Er, you boys have a licence?' I inquired.

The elder put the salmon's head back down on the ground.

'What's it to do with you?' he demanded truculently.

I sighed, and felt for my warrant.

'I'm a water bailiff . . . '

The tail joined the head on the ground as the younger boy rummaged in a chipped plastic sandwich-box containing a mass of knotted line, a broken trace, a couple of lures and various bits and pieces dear to the heart of a young fisherman. I felt like a bully; but then the boy found what he was searching for. It was tatty and the ink had blurred, but it established their legality. I thanked them and congratulated them, and watched them out of sight as they staggered along, the big fish hanging limply between them.

'That the first time you've come across the Wilson kids, Robbie?' said a familiar voice in my ear. I turned round to face George.

'Yeah – great couple of nippers. You should have seen the way they dealt with that salmon,' I said, and went on to tell him about the morning's events. ' . . . really incredible,' I finished. 'I feel quite jealous really. Why, I didn't catch my first salmon till I was in my twenties.'

George snorted in amusement.

'Yer greener than grass, Robbie boy. That's the third fish they've had out of this stretch since the holidays began and they've used that keep-net trick each time. Came out of that deep lie under the willows, did it? Thought so; favourite spot for springers, that. I s'pose they also told you they were taking the fish back to Mum?'

Whitethroat

I grimaced. 'Don't tell me; I can guess. The little villains are going straight to the fish-mongers.'

'Not quite. They told the truth – up to a point. What they didn't tell you is that Mum works in that new restaurant up the back o' town. With that last fish these lads must have a tidy sum tucked away in the post office.'

II

There are many reasons for working as a river warden or bailiff: there is the outdoor life, the companionship, the responsibility and the feeling of doing something useful – keeping a check on the environment, if you like. Speaking for myself, there are two other reasons, the first being the close contact and the opportunities for observation that the job affords me as a wild-life artist. As I walk the river banks, my subjects are all around me – in the trees, on the ground and in the water; birds, plants, insects, animals and fish, the rare and the common. Not so much a matter of seeking inspiration, but of trying to decide what not to paint!

The second reason is, of course, the fishing. Like many small boys I had a fascination for water and the creatures therein and that fascination has never departed. I may have graduated from a bent pin tied to a hazel switch with a length of string, to a hand-made cane fly-rod, but the attraction – the addiction – remains the same. From the moment of the first cast the angler's whole existence is concentrated upon the simple query, 'Will they, or won't they?'

Fishing satisfies the hunter in man but, unlike other forms of the chase, it is the quarry that dominates the sport not vice versa. Skill, subterfuge, experience and even luck are of little avail against fish that won't take the bait. The much-vaunted perks of fishing, the fresh air, the scenery, peace and tranquillity, are little more than a pleasant bonus when it comes to the nitty-gritty; an angler requires the same concentration and dedication whether he be fishing for perch in an old industrial canal or stalking big brownies in a Hampshire chalk-stream. Whether the fish is destined for the table or to be returned to the water is of little consequence; the reward comes in having outwitted him, in having persuaded him that your bait or lure is every bit as delicious as any of the more natural meals floating in or on the water, and then to have successfully played and landed him.

Those who denigrate fishing tend to the view that the fish is a cold-blooded primitive of limited intelligence; maybe so, but the beast is far from stupid – it has evolved a very sensitive set of reflexes which, coupled with a highly developed sense of self-preservation, makes it a worthy adversary. A fish also has an ability to learn (although some learn faster than others) and it is also extremely unpredictable.

All anglers have their favourite waters. Predictably, I suppose, mine is the river that I live beside and for which I am responsible: the river Walkham. It is not a big river, being little over fifteen miles in length, but its character is dictated by its origins and its nature is as changeable as the land of its origin. Dartmoor acts as a huge natural sponge and when saturation point is reached the idyllic tinkling stream can become, in a matter of hours, a swollen and destructive fury of muddy foaming water, capable of smashing fallen trees and moving huge boulders as if they were pebbles. The torrent can subside as suddenly as it arrived; the only evidence of its passing being the opaque silted waters, and the grasses, twigs and leaves on the bank – detritus of the spate – swept into a regimented line, evidence of a high-water mark several feet above the norm.

The water was just beginning to clear after such a spate on the

Salmon studies

126

scale section

Salmon studies
Woodtown 27.9.47

Head of adult male
in spawning livery

day that I met the Thinking Man's Salmon. I had been up since about four in the morning, having been called out along with several of my colleagues in a fruitless search for poachers reportedly netting on the lower reaches of the Tamar. Observation of the area produced nothing nor did a search of both banks which lasted from daybreak until well after midday. No tyre tracks, foot-marks, scales or equipment. A hoax or diversion? Nobody knew or cared by the time we were dismissed and sent home, cold and weary. I changed and had something to eat, but by then sleep no longer seemed so inviting and I decided to spend a couple of hours of my unexpected free time fishing.

It was early spring, cool and wet, and the initial run of fish had been disappointing; good catches had been reported further to the east on the Dart and Teign, but for some reason or other 'our' salmon were being remarkably backward in coming forward. I made my way to a stretch above Double Waters where a series of deepish pools are joined by a small waterfall or chute known as the Soda Syphon. Pale sunshine shone on water the colour of clouded bitter as it pushed and hurried its way to union with the Tavy further downstream. They were ideal spinning conditions, so I decided to use a small silvery Vibrex spoon, starting at Burrows' Pool and then working my way downstream. My rod was a little stiff for the light lure and initially I had some difficulty in covering the water; because of overhanging branches, the only form of casting possible was a sideways flick from the bank. I was on my third or fourth retrieval, and on the point of changing the lure to a heavy Devon, when the fish struck. No gentle, inquiring nibble, no tentative tug, no puzzled pull; there was nothing to presage a sudden and sustained heave accompanied by that most magic of sounds as line is torn from the drum of a reel under load; so much load, in fact, that I almost dropped the rod under the impact. I was just recovering when I received a second shock; having stripped at least ten feet off the reel, the fish headed upstream, snatching at the slack as it passed me at speed. Now, usually a salmon, and I couldn't imagine what else could have taken the bait with such authority, will swim downstream, heading back the way it came to safety. Not this one. The line slackened again as the fish neared the head of the pool, then appeared to fall back with the current. Three times this happened, up to the head of the pool and back, and if I tried to apply anything but the lightest tension on the line there was a firm resistance. In anticipation of a small springer I had brought only light tackle, but this felt like a king among fishes, and on the fourth run up I saw him; there, just inches under the surface of the clouded flow, and trailing a hummocked wake, was the pale but unmistakable outline of a huge salmon. Once more at the head of the pool, he merely turned broadside to the current and let it take him effortlessly and rapidly downstream again. He was facing me as he passed and the odd thought popped into my mind that perhaps he was considering how to play *me!* I applied a gentle sidestrain and immediately the massive head shook in the negative and another few feet of precious line screeched off the reel. To my horror he just kept on going with the sluicing stream – through the tail of the pool, the shallows and rocks and into the next stretch. Frantically, I chased after, rod in one hand upheld over the river, while the other fended off branches and brambles. It was hard going, and at every check the heavy fish took more line. By the time I had covered less than a hundred yards, I had lost my hat, filled one wader with water (idiotically, I had forgotten to roll them up after crossing the fields to the river), and my face and left hand looked as if I had been trying to deal with an angry wild-cat. Ignoring the scratches and squelches I stumbled on, the salmon remaining all the while firmly in control. In the stretch before the water-chute he repeated his earlier tactic and I decided to take advantage of his upstream absence to cross over the rocks to the other bank, which was clearer. It was at that very moment, straddled uncertainly over the throat of the fall, that I realized who was in charge. The line went suddenly slack and through the sliding column of water dashed the silvery-blue form of the fish – straight between my legs! He landed with a tremendous splash in the pool below and headed down-stream at speed. I swung my leg over the line, very nearly emulated the fish's performance, and stumbled after in clumsy pursuit. Several times he waited for me to catch up, reeling in as best I could, then off he would go again, towing his near-crazed angler behind. My heart was hammering like a road-drill for the salmon was quite the biggest I had ever hooked into; I estimated his weight at well over twenty pounds; gargantuan for our little river. His behaviour, however, continued to puzzle me – I would class myself as a moderately experienced salmon fisherman, yet this fish was acting in a manner I had never encountered. There was no frantic effort to rid himself of the hook, no desperate convulsions to com-bat the check of the line; his tactics were more or less effortless, principally using his mass and the power of the current to keep me at bay. He was no tired spent kelt for I had seen the sea-lice clearly on his steely-blue flanks as he had rushed through the chute.

Pools, shallows, riffles and rock-strewn narrows – on we went. It seemed as if we wouldn't stop until the fish had towed me past Ply-mouth Breakwater! The power of the beast was startling. Twice I applied additional drag, and twice the small rod bowed and creaked in protest as the line came humming taut, but still the fish, with little additional effort, was able to strip line. My forearms ached with the effort of trying to keep the rod at the correct angle and by now both waders were almost full of water. What was even worse, I had lost my tailer somewhere along the path of desperate pursuit; now I had little hope of landing the monster. I snatched a moment to look around. Not a soul in sight. The only chance was to beach the fish, but this was precluded by the fact that the banks had been severely undercut by the recent flooding. All I could do was to stand and make a fight of it; risk the tackle and losing the fish for the chance of establishing dominance. My moment came as the salmon headed upstream again. Gasping with effort I hurled myself after him, reeling in savagely and applying sidestrain to bring him closer. There was an instant reaction as before but I clamped my palm on the drum as tight as I dared. Almost immediately, the pull ceased as the fish turned and swam back towards me. I reeled in frantically as the fish headed for the deeper water close to the bank a little downstream from me. There was a moment's confusion and perhaps my reactions were not as they should have been, for I lost some additional line. Then, to my astonishment, the fish reappeared in the pebble-strewn shallows not three feet from me, his dorsal fin standing almost wholly clear of the water. He was quite the most beautiful cock-fish I had ever seen. A steely silvery-blue torpedo, he lay in the water almost quiescent, showing little sign of exertion – the only evidence being the little metallic spoon in the corner of his curving jaw. His tail flicked lethargically and I realized that something was very wrong; I had the rod well up and the line tight – but there was no movement, no give, no pull. The line was obviously caught on something. There seemed to be only one course of action. I pulled out a handkerchief and took a cautious step towards the huge fish. He didn't appear to notice. I bent down, handkerchief in hand, to grasp his tail. The moment my hand touched all hell broke out; a convulsive wriggle sent a sheet of water all over me and that, coupled with the impact of his powerful hindquarters against my wrist, sent me staggering backwards to sit with a painful bump in some ten inches of water. Net result: soaked angler, smashed rod-tip, broken line and lost fish – I had never even seen him go.

I looked at my watch. The whole episode had taken just under an hour, although it seemed much shorter; and I suppose we must have covered nearly half a mile of river, although it seemed much

Shaggy Ink Cap, or Lawyer's Wig *(Coprinus camatus)*

Robin Armstrong

longer. I salvaged the remains of my tackle, if not my pride, and started the uncomfortable walk back. A pigeon clattered out of the trees above and in the fields beyond the woods I could hear the tremulous murmur of sheep. Further down the river came a splash; a mocking, almost challenging, great galumph! of water. But it was not for me; I know when I've had enough . . .

III

That was the most memorable of all the fish that ever got away, but it's true to say that in some instances they were never there in the first place. Take the case of the phantom sea trout. Sea trout, or peal, fishing at night is, I think, the classic form of West Country angling. To be beside the river on a still June night listening to the occasional splash of the peal as they make their way upstream is my idea of sheer heaven.

Admittedly, the night of the phantom fish was nowhere near such romantic perfection; it was raining with dreary persistence and gusts of wind were making casting difficult – not that it's easy at night anyway. I was using a rather sparsely tied Butcher and working the fly gradually downstream. There were fish around – I had scouted the spot earlier in the day and had heard one or two hopeful splashes – so there seemed a fair chance of something for the table. Twenty minutes and a slight tangle later I felt a tentative tug followed almost immediately by a solid pull. I struck and battle royal commenced. The pool was not long and shelved rapidly at its lower end and I was determined to keep the peal firmly in check and to play him only in the deeper water. To begin with, his attempts to escape downstream were unimpressive but as I brought him closer his efforts redoubled, and I began to wonder if I had not hooked a salmon by chance. His rushes were of short duration but tremendously powerful, particularly in the deeper waters of midstream. It was a hard-fought battle, the only accompaniment being the magic song of the reel. Then, just as I was unclipping my landing net the fish took another rush downstream, appeared to turn at the shallows and then bang! he was gone. Dispiriting to say the least since he seemed to be a fair weight.

I carried on fishing for another half-hour or so but with no joy – the wind was getting up and it was becoming increasingly difficult to get more than a few feet of line out. Besides, having lost a leader and fly once, I was reluctant to hazard further tackle in such uncertain conditions. Once again, I returned home fishless but without even the consolation of having seen my adversary.

Three days later I was working about half a mile downstream from where I had been fishing. Pollution had been reported; something to do with a slurry tank being emptied into a drainage leat. George and Bob, a fellow-bailiff from the Tamar, who not only are my superiors but also possess the inestimable advantage of having known the area and its inhabitants since childhood, were of the opinion that the whole matter was probably a wild goose chase. Something to do with a feud between two neighbouring farming families.

'Tis one o' they vendetty things,' said Bob, a trifle obscurely. 'Buggers ain't spoke since the Coronation.'

Still, a complaint had been made, so we religiously inspected every leat ditch and stream in the area, putting water samples into little bottles for analysis by the Water Authority. Halfway through this process we became aware that we had an audience, a short, mean-featured man with a grease-stained felt hat. He had about him all the appearance of an agricultural tramp, yet when he spoke his accent was well educated, if abrupt.

'That's right. Samples. Prove it for once and for all. Prosecute. Only way to deal with people like that.'

George, I noticed, was eyeing the little man with distaste.

'I thought it might be you that complained, Captain. Why didn't you leave your name when you called?'

'What's it to do with you? Just get on and do your job. Tax-payer. Pay for you lot. Disgraceful,' came back the offensive if somewhat cryptic reply.

George glanced heavenwards. 'All right, then – but have you any idea where this slurry's supposed to be?'

'Course. Saw it. That ditch over there. Leads to the leat. Disgusting. Typical of that family. No better'n bloody tinkers.'

George's eyebrows drew together. 'Look,' he said evenly, we've been to the farm and they say the whole story is rubbish, just malicious gossip – that's all. And what's more,' he added, as the little man opened his mouth, 'my colleagues and I have just walked the entire length of that ditch and the leat, an' if there's any pollution then I'm a Dutchman. No tractor's been near there for days.'

'Doubting my word? Impertinence. Report you. All of you. Incompetents. Oafs. Wh-why,' he stammered in rage, 'known this place all m-my life. Know it better th-than me own backside . . . '

''An' when was the last time you saw that?' asked Bob, sweetly.

Threats of complaint, of dismissal, of influence in high places followed. George indicated that we should move on, with a nod of his head, and we left the strange fellow shrieking abuse among the sloping pastures. We collected the box of samples and made our way back to the land-rover along the river bank.

'Fair mazed,' said Bob, tapping his forehead significantly. 'Calls hisself a captain – what of I should like to know? He weren't no Navy man, an' if'n he were in the Army then it weren't our mob. Mind you, the other lot aren't much better,' and he indicated the tumbledown farm buildings we had visited earlier. 'If it's not one lot complainin' then it's the other. Hate each other, they do. Terrible way to live.' And Bob, a peaceable man, shook his head and sighed.

'But what's it all about?'

'Nobody knows; least of all they buggers. Prob'ly all in their imagination; deluded-like.'

We walked on in silence reflecting on the bitter enemies forced to live as neighbours in the remote little valley, with the original subject of their contention long forgotten.

'Here,' said George, dropping to his knees by the bank, 'give us a hand, Robbie.'

I knelt down and looked over the under-cut edge, and there, wedged tightly among the roots, was a familiar-looking 'No Fishing' sign.

'Must have been washed down from Grenofen bridge in the last spate. Pop it in the back and we'll nail it up again.'

I took the painted plywood and moved towards the land-rover. Something black and silver and red caught my eye, something that was deeply embedded in the wood, something that trailed a length of four-pound breaking strain monofilament – a sparsely-tied Butcher. Feuding farmers, it would seem, were not the only ones to be 'deluded-like'.

IV

The old Olympic ideal of honourable competition finds an echo in many an angler's heart. We have all lost fish, snagged driftwood,

broken tackle, and suffered the frustration of knowing the fish were there and yet being unable to persuade them of the superior attractions of rod-attached bait *versus* the more natural variety. It's a competition between two different species with the honours fairly evenly distributed. Of course it is pleasant to win (no matter whether the fish is to be returned to the water or borne home in triumph) but the primary satisfaction lies in inveigling the fish to take part.

The river warden or bailiff is doubly fortunate in that during the open seasons he spends much of his time simply patrolling the bank, answering queries, investigating complaints and checking licences and permits–the more public aspect of the job. In that manner one is fortunate to watch other anglers at their sport and to learn from their triumphs and tragedies. The shared enjoyment of a common interest makes fishing the most democratic of pastimes; since I have been working beside the river I can honestly say that I have seen a dustman instruct a duke in the intricacies of the Spey cast and a retired admiral patiently revealing to an unemployed teenager the secrets of his own variation on the blood-knot.

After a while the 'customers' become more than fellow-fishermen; a casual conversation about, say, the merits of the Peter Ross over the Alexandra or the advantages of fixed-spool over multiplier, can often diverge into more personal and esoteric fields; atomic theory and the tuning of a racing motorcycle being just two of the subjects I have been told about by experts. The fact that I understood little of either didn't really seem to matter. Acquaintance often ripens into friendship that goes far beyond the realms of the river bank.

It has been said that West Country game fishing when compared with the classic fisheries of the rest of England, Wales and Scotland is not dissimilar to the difference between rough-shooting and driven shooting. Like all such statements it is of a sweeping nature, but there is definitely something about our tree-lined rough-and-tumble waters that seems to attract some of the most colourful characters.

We are often asked, times being what they are, if we catch any female poachers and the answer is 'not as such', for on the rare occasions that women have ended up before the bench, they have generally been charged in the role of accomplice. However, when it comes to the legitimate side of angling there are many women who can more than hold their own against the men; it is worth remembering that the British rod-caught record for a salmon is sixty-four pounds and that this enormous fish was caught by a Miss Ballantyne on the Tay as long ago as 1922. There are a number of extremely fine female anglers who fish our rivers regularly and few of them answer to the popular image of the tweedy, hearty country-woman. When I first started as a warden there was one woman in particular whose accent was so upper class that I could never understand her – until things went wrong. She would arrive beside the river in her Barbour and fish away neatly and skilfully with never a hair out place. I was always worried that she would ask me some technical question about fishing that I simply wouldn't be able to understand. However, I used to hang around just in case things went wrong for her – like losing a fish, snagging a bough or, for all we knew, breaking a nail. For then all hell would be let loose – and that was probably the mildest word in her vocabulary. Gone was the affected drawl; in a crystal-clear voice set at about a thousand decibels, she would curse and swear in the most spectacular manner.

George, who is a Methodist, would shake his head gloomily and mutter: ''Tisn't right, 'tisn't right at all.' Bob, who is rather more earthy, would listen in open admiration, saying to himself: 'That's what I call powerful swearin', that is.' As a Cockney, I had heard it all before; but never with such conviction, clarity and volume. The only thing that surprised me was that the river didn't boil, or the bank catch fire; certainly her fellow-anglers would edge away in apprehension of some supernatural disaster, but, like a summer squall, the riveting language would soon die away and within moments she would be her old sunny, composed self, flicking her line smoothly across the water to land within millimetres of target.

No doubt about it: passions can run high where fishing's involved. It is not always the peaceful and contemplative art of popular fiction. I have seen rods broken in rage and frustration, tears shed and experienced tension and stress worthy of Hitchcock at his best. I have seen a peer of the realm felled by a punch that Henry Cooper would have been proud to acknowledge (it was delivered by his irate wife because he was late for lunch after a morning's trout fishing) and I have seen a man so depressed and distracted by his lack of success on the water that, unthinkingly, he engaged reverse instead of forward in his brand-new Volvo estate and drove smartly into the river.

V

Under the provisions of the Salmon and Freshwater Fisheries Act, wardens are responsible for the game fish of the area, i.e. salmon and trout. But the South West offers great fishing of another kind –

sea-angling. Personally, I am devoted to any form of fishing (my wife says I would dangle a line in a teacup if nothing else was available) but the sea-angling over the rocky and wreck-strewn bottom is superb. I think I am right in saying that nearly 50 per cent of the United Kingdom rod-caught records have been taken on or around these shores. I can certainly vouch for one of these records, for I hold it. Armstrong's claim to fame rests on the capture of an inoffensive little fish resembling nothing so much as a stunted cod – to which it is indeed related. This is the pouting, or pout-whiting, or perhaps more impressively *Trisopterus luscus* of the family Gadidae. My specimen weighed in at five pounds eight ounces and was nearly a pound heavier than the previous record-holder. For those who are interested it was caught from aboard the good ship *Tuonela* fishing out of Paignton, and was taken on a bait of squid suspended from a Clements boom. The date of this earth-shaking event was 10 August 1969 and the place was a mile to the south-east of Berry Head. (Now comes the confession; at the time I was trying for a conger.) Pouting are by no means an uncommon fish, and in fact some sea-anglers consider them to be a downright nuisance particularly around rocks and wrecks.

I had first been introduced to the pouting by a splendid character I met on Dungeness beach many years ago. Old Jack or 'Tap-Tap' (named after the double nudging inquiry of the pouting before taking the bait) swore blind that they were the 'greatest sport ever' – and indeed, if it wasn't for him, I doubt whether my name would be in the British record books, now, for that magnificent

'My' pouting

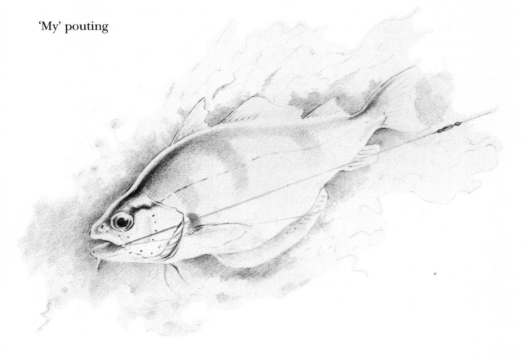

specimen would probably have been consigned to the deep and the search for conger would have continued. However, 'Tap-Tap' caught me at an impressionable age; the age at which, no matter what the interest, enthusiasm turns to mania, and technical information is hoarded with passion. I subscribed to every angling magazine going and sent off for every catalogue in print. I knew everything about everything – or thought I did – and never moved without a custom-built rod case and a tackle-box the size of a sea-chest. So when my pouting first broke surface on a flat-calm brassy summer's day in the English Channel, I knew at first sight I had hooked a record. From the encyclopedia of fishing ephemera stored in my mind I retrieved the fact that the present British record had stood at four pounds ten ounces since 1935. I nearly fainted with excitement at the sight of my fish swimming lethargically on the end of my line. I was fortunate in my companions – Ewan Clarkson, the writer, and Allan Bingle, the experienced skipper of the boat – for there is a very strict procedure for registering a record catch. The weighing scales have to be surrendered to the Inspector of Weights and Measures for calibration, the fish dispatched to a marine laboratory for official identification, and endless forms to be filled in and witnessed. I was like a train-spotter who has just seen the 'Comet' pull into platform three at Waterloo. Who on earth was going to believe me? Eventually a letter arrived from the British Record Rod-Caught Fish Committee. I was, and still am, a record-holder.

Looking back on it, I realize that I was just plain lucky. Old Jack had made the pursuit of the pouting his lifetime's work, and there I was, in my early twenties, hauling up the biggest pouting ever seen in British waters – and for all I know, the world – by sheer luck. Still, luck's an essential ingredient in angling, and much as I would like to say that it was all due to skill and perseverance, I will never forget that moment. If you've ever wondered what it must be like to win the pools, I can tell you this much – it can't be half as much fun as catching a little fish that resembles a stunted cod and weighs a mere five pounds eight ounces.

VI

As wardens, we exist primarily to serve the public, principally in their role as anglers. I can think of no better way to illustrate this or, indeed, to demonstrate the fidelity of Walton's 'Brotherhood

Hooked brown trout

138

Robin Amstrong

of the Angle', than by recounting the story of George and the Brigadier.

The Brigadier was one of that vast number of men who had retired to west Devon after a lifetime spent 'Out East'. He was Indian Army, the last of several generations, and with the partition of India he found himself redundant, with the minutest of pensions. His family had once owned large estates in the Tavistock area, although by the time he returned there was little or nothing left. Notwithstanding, he bought a miner's cottage, mean and derelict, beside the Tavy and spent some of his hard-earned gratuity on doing it up. He settled in with his wife and two sons, devoting his now abundant free time to public service of all kinds: he was on the Bench, the Council, the Playing-Fields Committee, the Education Committee, and heaven knows what else. Just how he coped on his pittance nobody knew, but he was always there for help and advice. No stereotyped do-gooder or Colonel Blimp he, just an old-fashioned English gentleman of the very best sort. The only luxury he allowed himself was fishing, a sport he had pursued all his life and at which he was adept.

The Brigadier was well on in years when I came to work beside the river, and age and infirmity had forced him to give up the majority of his voluntary work, but his tall stooping figure was still a familiar sight along the banks. His step was somewhat uncertain but he could still throw a pretty line, if not quite so far as in his earlier years. He was a great favourite with us all, and it was considered something of a privilege to be invited into his garden, with its immaculate borders and rows of tall staked flowers, for a 'cup o' char and a chat'. He was no fishing bore, for in truth he had that rare ability of being able to listen and encourage conversation.

George was the closest to him, for I believe they had regimental connections and I know for a fact that he had taken the Brigadier's sons fishing ever since they were small. Then came the sad day when his wife died and for a while the 'Brig' vanished from the scene. George told us that he had gone to visit his sons who had followed in their father's footsteps and joined the Army. Both had families of their own now, in Germany and Aldershot, and we wondered if perhaps the old man would move in with either of them. He was obviously welcome for he was away for a considerable time, but then George's wife who had been keeping an eye on the little cottage got a letter; the old boy would be back for the beginning of the season.

When he returned we had a shock. The tall and stooping figure was now bent and wraith-like, his movements hesitant; worse, his eyesight was failing rapidly. It seemed as if he would soon follow his beloved wife.

'Dunno as how th'old feller can cope,' said Bob, some three days before the start of the season. 'I went past the cottage this mornin' an' there he was with that old greenheart, practisin' castin' on the lawn, like. Missin' the target by miles he were, an' didn't even seem to know it. 'Tis a terrible shame if'n a lovely old gent like the Brig won't be able to go fishin' next Saturday.'

We looked at George but he seemed strangely unconcerned as he munched on a sandwich and rolled silver-foil taken from the carpark litter bin into a ball.

'Collectin' fer charity agin?' asked Bob, nodding at this activity. 'What's it this time? Guide-dogs or something?'

'Something,' said George thickly through a mouthful of cheese-and-pickle, and helped himself to the cooking foil in which Bob's pasty lay.

There were the usual last-minute preparations for the season with a couple of anti-poaching patrols thrown in for good measure, and so it was not until the early evening of the second day that I met up with Bob again.

'Doin' anything, Robbie?' he asked. I told him that I was just going off duty, having been up since three that morning. ''Nother half-hour or so won't matter, m'dear. Brigadier's goin' fishin' agin.'

'Again? I thought the old chap could hardly see?'

Bob grinned, and held open the car door. 'He can't, least not very well, but I'll tell you this much: th'old feller had two handsome little brownies yesterday. Near a pound apiece.'

That, for our acid waters with their paucity of nourishment, was handsome indeed. We parked the car and walked across the fields to the small cottage and along the side of the garden hedge to the river. Just as we were about to turn the corner, Bob motioned to me to stop and indicated that I should look cautiously around the hedge. The river flows past the Brigadier's house in a broad shallow stretch broken only by a few rounded boulders that jut smoothly from the surface. It is not a place where salmon or peal tarry, but the little brown trout seem to like it and their spotted shadowy forms dart among the riffles.

There, in the middle of this stretch, supported by a shooting stick firmly wedged against one of the boulders, was the Brigadier. He reminded me powerfully of a slightly moth-eaten old heron as he sat there motionless in midstream.

'What's he . . . '

'Ssh!' said Bob, and pointed to the other side of the bank where, slightly downstream from the Brigadier, lurked George on his hands and knees. As we watched, the old man began to false-cast. When he had got some twenty-five feet of line whistling smoothly through the air, George called out softly, 'Enough!'

'Righto, George,' replied the Brigadier placidly, continuing to keep the line in motion under the soft whippy power of the ancient greenheart rod. 'Say when . . .'

George put out his hand and released a bright silvery ball on to the water. As it floated downstream George watched it carefully for a moment, then said 'Now!' Almost immediately, the fly-line flicked out and the cast dropped neatly behind the ball of silver-foil. The old man worked the flies across the stream deftly, then slowly recovered line. Three times the process was repeated, and on the fourth cast, the trout, who must have been mesmerized by the bombardment of silver-foil giving away its position, succumbed. Minute though the fish was, it was evident from the old man's expression that its capture gave him as much pleasure as the mahseer and Himalayan brook trout of his youth. He and George stood together admiring the speckled little fish as it lay in the net.

'That was splendid, George, absolutely splendid. Pop him back in and come and have a whisky to celebrate.'

We left quietly, leaving George to help the old man ashore. We walked back in silence, until Bob, clearing his throat, said, 'Cunnin' old sod. Mind, 'tis a terrible example for a senior bailiff to set, litterin' the ol' Tavy like that.' And he winked.

Coot

CHAPTER SEVEN

...AND FOUL

I

xiv.   A bailiff should always try to avoid bringing about an assault on himself. Many offenders turn nasty when asked to stop, be searched, allow seizure, etc. Hours of talking are always better than seconds of fighting. Never do or say anything to provoke an assault. If assaulted do no more than you consider necessary to defend yourself and to prevent a further assault.

SWWA Notes to Wardens

THE tide was ebbing fast and before our tired and burning eyes dark humps of mud began to appear on the silvery surface of the moonlit estuary, and the wide stretch of water began to recede to what would eventually become a winding narrow river twisting its way between the exposed silt, reeds and salt marsh. The last of the cold rain squalls had forced its unwelcome attentions on us some minutes earlier; the blinding, stinging rain lashing across the slopes brought an almost welcome relief from the paralysing numbness that steals over one with the onset of exhaustion.

That was the third night spent beside the estuary, and the seventh in a fortnight. Some of Them had been spotted in the neighbourhood and They were not going to poach our territory – at least not if we could help it.

I blinked and tried to focus on the dark waters. The insides of my eyelids felt as if they were coated with sandpaper, and it was only with an effort that I forced them open again. The more tired you are the slower time seems to pass. A dark blob had appeared in midstream moving slightly faster than the outgoing tide, the wake showing as a series of V-shaped ripples in the milky-white light of the moon. It was a common seal in search of a late supper – salmon. But our quarrel was not with his kind but with fish-thieves of the two-legged sort.

The passage of the seal disturbed some stiff-legged waders on the mud-flats and there was an agitated twittering of sound as they jerkily closed ranks. Then it was the turn of the seal to be alarmed. His smooth passage through the water suddenly slowed and his blunt head came higher, searching for sound and movement that were inaudible and invisible to me. Then he was gone, with just the faintest of shadowed ripples to indicate his passing. Simultaneously, the speaker of my radio gave a double click – the agreed signal for someone unknown approaching. Fatigue was replaced by apprehension.

I felt my heart beginning to thump and sought by surreptitious movements to loosen my stiffened legs. I tried to remember the positions of the other bailiffs: George on the bank opposite, home in his beloved Cornwall, Dave and Bob both on the same side as myself but higher up and further downstream. I could hear nothing except the muted high sounds of the birds and the rustle of the breeze among the leaves. The radio clicked twice again. Whoever it was was too close to the unknown intruders to risk speech transmission – the clicking sound was made by simply depressing the transmit button. Still nothing. Worse, the breeze was colder on the face and the ripples on the water were sharper and more acute shadows; another squall was on the way, depriving us of what little visibility we had.

Suddenly there was a light to my left, a powerful beam that shone across the river and wavered. There were shouts and a muffled crackling on the radio. I ran towards the sound, slipping on the greasy steepness of the bank. An engine revved loudly, tyres spun on loose gravel, the light swung across me. In the moment before its glare blinded me, I realized that it was the double headlights of a car. There was another revving and roaring followed by a metallic crash, then the sound of a vehicle being driven away at considerable speed.

The radio gave another of its semi-intelligible burbles and I realized that Dave was reporting the vanishing car.

'... white Cortina estate, licence number romeo july yankee ...' He sounded shaken, even through the hiss of static.

When I eventually reached the scene I found that Bob had got there before me and was tending to a battered Dave by the gentler light of a torch. Little wonder he had sounded shaken. Bleeding profusely from a nasty-looking gash on the head, he was leaning disconsolately against the crumpled wing of his own car which was lying slewed at an odd angle to the track. As Bob staunched the blood with a handkerchief, Dave continued his conversation on the handset – now evidently bringing a frustrated George up to date with developments.

' . . . four o'them. Came down the track with engine and lights off. I were just down the bank a touch an' never heard them arrive. They saw my ol' banger an' must have been a bit suspicious, like, but the first thing I heard was a door slamming so one of th' buggers must ha' got out for a look round. That's when I crept up to see what was going on . . . '

The radio gave an interrogatory squawk.

'No, 'course they didn't spot me. Anyway, my car must ha' put them off, for the driver got back in and started up. That's when I showed meself. Over.'

Another questioning crackle.

'Couldn't see, but it was our customers all right. The moment I stood up they took a bloody run at me, spun the car round, sideswiped mine and headed down the lane like a scalded cat.'

The voice through the atmospherics sounded vaguely concerned.

'Just a scratch where I ran into a tree. We'll wait for you here – can't go far in my car anyhow. Mind you don't forget yer passport crossing the bridge.'

The radio gave a final indignant splutter and fell silent. Dave had evidently recovered his sense of humour.

II

As we sat in the warmth of the damaged car and sheltered from the promised rain, conversation, which had centred on the escaped poachers, died away. Each of us reflected on what might have been. There are poachers, and then there are poachers . . .

Violence has long been part and parcel of the poaching world; stories of gamekeepers, bailiffs and poaching gangs fighting desperate battles in the dead of night have long been with us. In recent times, deliberate acts of violence have been fortunately rare – the majority of assaults have been committed in the heat of the moment, and any premeditated act has usually been in the form of vandalism; unpleasant, but endurable. Paint-throwing, damage to cars, or stones thrown through windows; generally the work of aggrieved locals who feel, in those immortal words, that they have been 'stitched up, loike'.

Poaching is big business, and what was once a cottage industry is now a multi-national. The real damage is caused not so much by the individual with the snare as by the well-organized and co-ordinated activities of the gangs.

There is nothing new about this; forty years ago, at a meeting of the Exe Board of Conservators, Sir John Amery made the following statement:

> 'It is no exaggeration to say that salmon poaching in the upper reaches has become very serious, and I think it has come about owing to the high price obtainable for the fish during the last two years. Those who have been watching the river estimate that over 500 salmon have been illegally taken from it . . . The poachers have even gone so far as to send the fish . . . to London. They have their own scouts, their own cars, they have their own men on the banks waiting and watching, and they have taken salmon openly in the middle of the afternoon.'

Sir John was talking about just one part of one river. Since 1945 there have been enormous changes in the administration, control and policing of the South West's rivers – yet this reorganization has only just kept pace with the problem of illegal fishing. Since the war years, the urban population has increased dramatically, the holiday trade has become an integral part of the area's economy and restaurants have proliferated, so that the demand for salmon has never been greater. Not for nothing is the fresh-run salmon known as the 'Bar of Silver' – and its value has more than kept pace with inflation.

The demand on the Continent is even greater; in 1984, good salmon was retailing in Belgium at around £15 per pound! When one considers that a well-planned poaching expedition can make in excess of £1000 for a night's work merely supplying local markets at around £4 per pound, then the scale of potential profits from a larger operation can be readily appreciated – and make no mistake, these large-scale operations do exist; the big poaching gangs are the bane of the countryside.

Naturally, these big gangs have had an effect on local poaching; the 'one for the pot and one for the pocket' mentality is long gone. After all, why should the locals restrict their activities when outsiders are making large sums of money at what used to be known as 'havin' a bit o' sport' – that is to say, popping down to a suitable stretch of river after the pubs close, producing a snare, gaff or snatch out of a pocket and taking a fish from under the noses of authority – *that's* where the sport lay, not in the taking of a fish

Swimming teal

(which is relatively simple by such methods) but in outwitting the wardens, bailiffs and keepers.

In a small rural community it is inevitable that we tend to know each other's business. We know the poachers and the poachers know us. It is the same strangely comfortable relationship that exists between the policeman and the small-time criminal. Each keeps an eye on the other, exchanges the same heavy-handed banter, and remains basically unconcerned—until one or the other party is out of sight.

For all the influence of the gangs it is surprising just how many of our locals react indignantly if their activities are compared with those of the 'professionals'. They are sentimentalists, fondly believing that they are still in it for 'the sport' when, in fact, they are merely dupes in the law of supply and demand. The philosophy of the pot and the pocket is obsolete; the pocket is all. Cash in hand and nothing to declare—in times of high unemployment, what could be more desirable?

The methods employed by the gangs owe nothing to the skills and finesse of the old-time poacher—not for them the patient acquisition of woodcraft, the intimate knowledge of each likely pool and the hard-learned experience of where a fish might lie; their methods have all the subtlety of a runaway tank. A recent example of such profitable vandalism was widely reported in the national press when three men were given twelve-month gaol sentences for poisoning a stretch of Welsh salmon river with the lethal chemical sodium cyanide, a small amount of which was sufficient to kill over 1800 'good-sized fish'—not to mention the eggs, alevin and parr that must also have perished, the salmon of future generations. That was the effect of just one pound of cyanide. The accused admitted to possessing over sixty pounds!

Such methods are not unknown in the South West; our rivers have also suffered from cyanide as well as lime, industrial bleach and even brake fluid. They all poison the fish and do untold harm to the environment.

As an indication of the scale and profits involved in these activities, a wide range of expensive and often sophisticated equipment has been confiscated by bailiffs and police over the years; inflatable boats, outboards, diving equipment (the wetsuit is almost *de rigueur* for the modern poacher), drums of chemicals, CB radios, camping equipment (including camper-vans, nothing like home comforts), spear-guns and nets. The modern man-made fibre net is far from cheap, and it is no coincidence that one of the principal poaching gangs in the south originate from the Dorset seaside town of Bridport, the country's net-making centre. The latest of these nets shows the astonishing advances made in this field in recent years – a sixty-foot drift-net with a six-foot 'hang' that, complete with floats, folds up into a package small enough to stow in an inside pocket!

Perhaps the most ingenious device captured so far was an adapted Jaguar car that had insulated tubes running from behind the headlights the length of the wings, and additional compartments under the rear passenger seats and in the boot. This remarkable vehicle was used for transporting fish to France within twenty-four hours of capture; unfortunately, the majority of salmon taken by the gangs leave the country apparently legally, 'fenced' through accommodating fish-merchants.

Mobility is of the essence for these gangs; for instance, certain members of the Bridport gang are well known to police forces throughout the United Kingdom. They may be on the Tamar and its tributaries this week and on the Wye or the Tweed the next. Nor do they confine their activities to salmon; game of every variety commands high prices and with nets, dogs, cross-bows and guns, they pursue their prey throughout the countryside. Deer, whether they be in sanctuary or woodland, are run down or shot, salmon taken in bulk by chemicals as drastic as Cymag, and game-birds netted and shot in their hundreds. Closed seasons are ignored and the slaughter is wholesale. Whether you be pro- or anti-blood-sports, town- or country-dweller is immaterial: the depredations of the big organized poaching gangs make us all the poorer.

III

In an effort to combat the damage caused by the gangs we have tried the wonders of modern technology, including image intensifiers (night 'scopes) and various electronic alarm systems, but their uses are limited, either because of budgetary considerations or impracticality. There is little advantage in being able to see at night unless you are in the same spot as the poachers, and little advantage in being able to detect movement along a river bank unless the equipment can tell the difference between, say, a man and a sheep. Such devices are no substitute for old-fashioned police work based on experience and judgment. If you know the area and its inhabitants then you have a solid basis from which to form an opinion on a likely course of action.

A good example of this 'deductive bailiffing' occurred just a few weeks ago. For all our reputation as one of the wettest areas in the country, it had been unnaturally dry for several months and the rivers were abnormally low. It was a serious situation for all, man and beast, but as the last of the scorching summer days faded with the coming of autumn, our natural climate began to reassert itself.

Far out over the grey waters of the North Atlantic, circulating polar air began to form itself into a massive depression heralded by a series of rain-bearing lows that swept over us from the south-west. The whole region gave a collective sigh of relief. In the drought, the rivers had become streams and the streams trickles, and the reservoirs revealed their submerged past: walls, foundations and even bridges showed themselves to a generation unaware of their existence. Notices abounded: 'Save Water Now', 'No Hosepipes' and, ominously, 'You are Entering a Drought Area'. With the coming of the rains, everything changed. Water butts and drinking troughs brimmed over, the last of the summer pastures began to take on a new freshness and lushness, and lambs, calves and foals destined for the autumn sales began to fatten before the eye. For one group of living creatures the rain brought not just relief but salvation – the salmon. The aberrant weather had endangered the autumn run; the fish had arrived in the estuary and moved from there into the wide lower reaches of their spawning rivers, but there they stayed for lack of water to help them on their tumbling, leaping journey in search of posterity. Good bailiffing is merely protecting the fish and its environment, and since the environment was dependent on the weather and therefore in the hands of the Almighty (who, contrary to popular opinion, does not sit on the board of the SWWA), the Fisheries and Recreation Department turned its attention to the salmon. Now the Water Authority's jurisdiction extends far beyond rivers – it also takes in the estuaries and the coastline to a distance some six miles out to sea. Since such an area is impossible to police with existing resources, attention is concentrated on those areas where the salmon are at greatest risk: the coastline closest to the estuaries, the estuaries themselves and the rivers.

The first controllable threat to the fish is to be found in the estuaries and their approaches: professional fishermen who are licensed to net salmon. Conditions are attached to the issuing of such licences and strictly control both the size and type of net employed and the times and places in which it may be used. To safeguard the fish while they waited in the lower reaches for the hoped-for spates, the SWWA took the unusual step of 'buying out' the netsmen – offering, in effect, compensation for their agreement

Common frog *(Rana temporaria)*, unfortunately no longer as common as they
used to be

to suspend activities. Further safeguards were introduced by
bringing forward the end of the open season, thus freeing the fish
from the attentions of all anglers and fishermen. There was a general consensus that the Authority was doing the right thing – true
fishermen are well aware of the necessity for conservation.

This left one problem – the poachers. With the fish amassing in
large numbers in the lower reaches they would have been easy prey
but for the corollary that their gathering in a limited area made
them equally easy to protect. The normal practice during a run
which can take place over a period of weeks is to mount almost
continuous patrols coupled with discreet observation of likely
poaching grounds. This autumn, though, it was almost easy. Our
main worries were not so much the poachers but that the fish
would become diseased through over-crowding or simply lack the

strength after their long fast to ascend the rivers. Fortunately the rains came just in time, and the run began. It was short, sharp and furious, almost as if the salmon, sensing that the future of their species hung precariously in the balance, were performing a piscatorial cavalry charge up the mud-stained torrents. The lack of visibility and the brief duration of the run made the poacher's task difficult and ours easier. We put in long hours but the rewards were worth it, although we will not know how successfully the fish bred for another year or so. My own personal satisfaction came from seeing the first fish arrive in the long pool below my cottage. There is a tall sequoia planted not far from the bank, and leaning against its reassuring bulk I had the pleasure of watching the silvery shadow of the hen-fish excavating her redd (nest) in the shallow and murky water.

An example like this shows the value of co-ordinated action in order to conserve fish stocks, and is perhaps bailiffing at its best. It also shows the worth of one central body–in this case the Fisheries and Recreation Department of the SWWA.

IV

Normally, trying to prevent poaching is similar to most forms of police work: a routine of patrolling and observation. Deterrence lies principally in establishing a known presence but it cannot be completely successful unless it is allied with arrest and prosecution; hence the need for good intelligence and patient groundwork that can come only from experience.

Previously I said that the public image of a bailiff often is a comic and bucolic one, and it is a regrettable fact that the same can be said of the poacher. I say regrettable because the image of the likeable village rogue tends to lessen the seriousness of the crime in the public's view–there is nothing likeable or romantic about the majority of modern poachers. Perhaps we should label that majority with the less appealing title of fish thieves and reserve the word 'poacher' with its rather more romantic connotations for those few characters for whom it *is* possible to have a sneaking admiration– even if one's sole ambition is to catch them in the act.

As far as 'local' offenders are concerned, they come in all shapes and sizes, ages and backgrounds. Their reactions on being apprehended are equally varied.

'I suppose I was overcome by the Evil Instinct.' Sixteen-year-old public schoolboy caught with large treble-hook snatch.

'I got them off a bloke in Tavistock, I don't know him, I've never met him before.' Ex-public schoolboy (several previous convictions for poaching) trying to sell snare-marked salmon to a wholesaler.

Q: 'Don't you think it is testing our intelligence a bit too far to expect us to believe that you have driven all the way down from Bridport to Totnes at 2.30 in the morning just for a drive?' A: 'No, not really, we often go for a drive like this.'

That exchange took place between a river warden and a member of the Bridport gang who had been caught with a fellow-poacher after a high-speed car chase. They were found guilty of two sets of offences on two different rivers on the same night. Although the first exchange is flippant, the most revealing remark came when the second suspect was questioned.

Q: 'You have two separate incidents against you on the same night and could find yourself with a prison sentence, especially if you continue to be uncooperative.' A: 'I can do time, I've done it before – it doesn't worry me.'

Then there was the defence used by a well-known poacher found in the river with a fork, the tines of which had been sharpened: 'We was rabbiting.'

'I never caught a fish in my life; I only came along for the boat-ride.' Illegal netsman.

'It couldn't have been me, I can't stand the feel of fish.' Another illegal netsman.

Warden: 'How come there are salmon scales in your haversack?' Poacher: 'I had fish-fingers for lunch.'

Warden: 'What's that sea trout doing on the floor of your car?' Poacher: 'I know you won't believe this, but I was stopped at the bridge admiring the view and enjoying the fresh air when the bugger jumped clean through the window.'

'I'm studying biology with the Open University.' Well-known poacher caught setting night-lines.

The excuses are endless and every bailiff has his own favourite. My own is rather special as it concerns one of the few poachers for whom I must admit a certain fondness since he is most definitely of the old school; it is also one of the few poaching stories ever to grace the pages of *Private Eye*. He was arrested by the river carrying a haversack containing a wetsuit, face-mask, torch, snare and gaff. His hair and trousers were wet, and there would have appeared more than 'reasonable grounds for suspicion'. However, when he appeared in court, it transpired that the real reason he had been in that particular boulder-strewn stretch of the Tavy was for the purposes of surfing. Having fallen off his board, he mislaid his vital St

Christopher from around his neck and thus required the face-mask to search for it. The snare was for rabbits and the gaff was in the haversack when he found it on a rubbish heap.

He was acquitted!

V

A week later. The Cortina that had so nearly run Dave over had been traced to an address in Dorset, not far from Bridport. Surprise, surprise. The owner when questioned said he had lent it to his brother for a fishing holiday. There was a good deal of teeth-sucking and sarcastic comment when this little gem was passed on. However, the car had not been returned and the owner denied all knowledge of his brother's whereabouts, didn't know or care when he would return, and, in the meantime would the police kindly go away and leave him alone – or words to that effect.

George decided we should try one more time. We had one big factor in our favour: the car-borrowing brother was an old customer with a long record of poaching offences – even better, he was cordially disliked in west Devon for his bullying behaviour. A barroom brawler with a vicious streak, he had reputedly laid out three local poachers with a broken bottle – hardly the most fraternal of acts. The car seemed to have disappeared without trace, but there was little difficulty in picking up the errant brother's trail, and his whereabouts was eventually established not far from the small village of Milton Combe, within easy distance of the estuary and all three principal rivers. His unpopularity led to reports coming in from every drinking establishment in the area. Local poachers of the more 'reputable' variety seemed to consider his presence an affront, and made no bones about it.

It was only fair that Dave, with three stitches in his forehead as a result of taking evasive action, should be the one to receive the definitive tip-off. Our Dorset friend, along with two of his compatriots and one of our less salubrious desperadoes, was going to make a final attempt – this time on the Tavy rather than the Tamar. Knowing their methods we felt sure that they would attempt to net the lower reaches; a deduction based on our first brief encounter, the area in which they were staying and the fact that the local member of the gang had once held a netsman's licence to operate in that stretch – until he became too greedy.

'Thursday it is,' reported Dave, and George took the gamble,

Turtle dove

hauling in fellow-bailiffs from as far as the Dart, on the eastern side of the moor, and the Fowey, where George claims he caught his first fish.

By ten o'clock that night there were ten bailiffs covering over a mile of river. The police had been alerted, and should the approach or escape be made from further downriver where the local gang-member kept his boat, the co-operation of the Ministry of Defence Police had been solicited. Their launch constantly patrolled the waters off Devonport naval base – not far from where the suspect craft was moored.

I remember thinking, as I settled down in the lee of a tumbled wall that ran out of the woodland and down to the foreshore, that to most people such preparations might smack of overkill – all this fuss and bother over a few petty criminals who were merely going to catch a few insignificant fish by illegal means; then I thought of how I might have been standing in Dave's place that cold and wet night just seven days ago. Maybe I wouldn't have moved so fast, and would have stood like a rabbit caught in the full gleam of the lights, terrified and indecisive, rooted to the spot just waiting helplessly for the final crunching impact. I shivered, even though the night was mild. Maybe the criminals weren't so petty after all.

Incongruously, the first few lines of 'The Lincolnshire Poacher' ran through my mind. ''Tis my delight in the shiny night in the season of the year.' I couldn't remember the rest, and anyway, wasn't he after pheasants or something? One thing was similar – it was certainly a 'shiny night', the moon reflecting palely on the mirrored surface of the water, thrown into relief by the dense blackness of the trees. Surely they wouldn't risk it a second time, not on a clear night like this?

Surprisingly, they did come, and I was hardly aware of the drama until it was nearly all over. The now familiar double click came over the radio, but hardly had my heartbeat begun to accelerate when there was a faint hiss of static and George's comfortable tones came on the air. It was all over and would all those on the east bank walk up to the old slipway?

I stood up and stretched. The sudden motion annoyed an oyster-catcher who took to the air in annoyance and skimmed into the darkness uttering what I presumed to be the most dire of threats. Further upriver I could see the uncertain beams of torches moving erratically; suddenly, I felt more cheerful. The poachers were, momentarily, no longer of consequence. The indignant bird, the familiar lap of the water, the still night with the stars twinkling familiarly overhead, the dusted brilliance of the Milky Way seemingly mirroring the north-south course of the river – for a brief, very brief moment I was back in the days when everything was all 'liddle birds and buttercups'.

A blue light flashed with startling regularity on the opposite bank – the cavalry had arrived. I made my way upriver, my boots making occasional loud 'sloops' in the quiet as I sank into the soft and clinging mud. It was, as the saying goes, all over bar the shouting. It appeared that the Cortina, still damaged after the dramatic events of last week, had been hidden not far from the scene of the dramatic getaway – its wing and steering making the vehicle almost unmanageable. The poachers had merely tucked it into a copse and continued their flight on foot.

After a couple of days they had cautiously visited the spot, since the rear of the car was filled with the tools of their trade, nets, wetsuits, waterproof torches, a smart inflatable dinghy and oars, and a packet of black plastic garbage bags. They could hardly believe their luck when they realized that we hadn't discovered their hiding place – but it was this good fortune that led to them becoming over-confident and making their presence felt in the neighbourhood.

None the less, we were lucky to have caught them. Fittingly, Dave was one of the arresting officers, and when I had eventually made my way to his side of the river – courtesy the inflatable dinghy making its last voyage before the bung was drawn and the little vessel impounded – he was preparing to leave for the police station.

'Same as before. Down the track, lights and engine off. Quiet as little mouses they were. Stopped over by the gate yonder, and started to inflate the dinghy an' change into they wetsuits right under our noses.'

I congratulated him.

'We was lucky, Robbie, dead lucky. Have a look in the back of the car.'

I shone my torch in the direction Dave indicated. The light reflected from small particles scattered seemingly at random over the tangle of nylon mesh, floats and paraphernalia. Scales. Salmon scales, by the look of them and still with the silvery sheen of the freshly caught rather than the milky opacity that comes later.

'Here, look at this little lot.'

Dave held open the mouth of one of the garbage bags. Six salmon, not one under ten pounds. A second sack held sea trout, more than a dozen of them, gleaming in the artificial light.

'Busy little so-and-so's. Must have been netting the pools higher up. Like I said, we were lucky.' He paused for a moment, listing the fish in his notebook, then added, somewhat regretfully, 'Didn't put up a fight, though. S'pose we must have taken them by surprise.'

I wandered back down to the river to see if I could give a hand and was instructed to search the ground carefully in case any piece of evidence might have been overlooked.

Six fish. Six chances for the future. A plastic garbage bag hardly seemed a dignified end for creatures who had come so far and who had so nearly achieved their goal. The years spent in the deep Atlantic avoiding the natural predators and the deep-sea trawlers' nets, the epic journey from the cold salt waters of the north to brave the hazards and perils of the shallower waters of the continental shelf and then the estuary; the metabolic shock of adjusting from sea-water to fresh; the self-imposed fast; the preparation for one last, desperate, stamina-sapping effort – all for nothing. Just the indignity of a bin-liner for a shroud.

I crunched over a muddied patch of shingle and the light from my torch flicked over a littered assortment of jetsam – a beer can, an empty container for washing-up liquid, a cork float and, bobbing gently in the current as if uncertain whether to continue or not, a salmon. Not a shining bar of silver but a pathetic wasted corpse, a kelt. The colour gone, the fungus rampant, the kippered fish seemed an obscene parody of those magnificent creatures lying in the plastic bag just a few yards away.

Yet there was hope in his death for he had spawned, had fertilized the eggs of a future generation, and had exhausted his bodily resources in the effort. Now his spent corpse drifted seaward in the dark waters.

I wondered how many of his fellows had found the same fulfilment.

Perhaps one of the saddest sights in nature: a magnificent cock salmon lying dead
after defending the redd. I pick these up every year and bury them

NOTES ON THE PAINTINGS

Here are some notes on the methods and equipment that I have found satisfactory over the years (with the exception of official notebooks!).

SKETCHING. I now use Daler sketchblocks, pocket-sized, and 1B pencils made by Venus – although I have to confess that I often resort to a ball-point or felt-tip when the weather is damp. Since I can rarely choose my own time for sketching (that I reserve for painting proper) the conditions are often inclement, and unless a very soft pencil is used there is a strong likelihood of tearing the paper. I have tried plastic-coated notebooks given to me by a sailing friend and found them excellent, since they can be used with an ordinary pencil. Unfortunately, they were American and I have not been able to get replacements.

WORKING-UP. This is the term I use for preparing the final study for painting. I work directly on to tracing paper, so that when I have achieved a satisfactory result I can transfer it directly on to the watercolour paper. Although I use my own studies as the basis of a picture, coupled with observations of the surrounding environment, etc., I will happily make use of photographs I have taken. For the fine detail which suits my particular style, only a photograph can 'freeze' what is normally an elusive and rapidly moving subject. The great Victorian artists, lacking the 35mm camera and its flexibility, made much use of the taxidermist. That, too, is a technique that I have used for detail, and I would like to pay tribute to the help and kindness shown to me by the Natural History Department of the County Museum at Exeter.

PAINTING. In my experience, it is a sad truism – sad because of the expense – that the best results come only from the best materials, and I have experimented for a number of years to find those best suited to me. The paints and brushes are both made by Rowney. For detailed work I prefer their 'Diana' range of sable brushes – they seem to last longer than any others I have tried.

The paper I use is hand-made, a heavy cotton linter which is tinted with an iron oxide dye to my specification, and is made by Sheepstor Hand-made Paper Ltd at Yelverton, not five miles from where I live. This impressive-sounding company is a one-man business run by an energetic fellow named Tim Powell who operates out of his garage which is full of the most splendid gadgetry, including enormous cast-iron presses and enough vats and cauldrons to stock a witches' supermarket. The results are superb.